Reminiscences of

Vice Admiral Ruthven E. Libby

U.S. Navy (Retired)

U.S. Naval Institute

Annapolis, Maryland

1984

Preface

The oral history of Admiral Libby has a number of interesting aspects for the benefit of historians studying the events in which he participated. Judging by the detail with which he discussed them, Admiral Libby evidently recalls his destroyer squadron commands of World War II with considerable interest. He commanded Destroyer Squadron One in the Aleutians campaign, which was fought in miserable weather, and then he moved on to the Central Pacific campaign for a raid on Wake Island and the Gilbert Islands operation. After taking command of DesRon 56, a new squadron, he was involved in shore bombardment training and the invasions of the Marianas and the Palau group.

His shore service during the war is also bound to be worthy of study, because he began the war as an aide to Admiral Ernest J. King, moving with King from the Atlantic Fleet to the U.S. Fleet command (CominCh). As a close insider, Admiral Libby was in position to judge Admiral King's reputation as a hard-nosed naval officer. Libby concludes that the people who thought of King in those terms were the men whose work didn't satisfy the admiral. Near the end of the war, Admiral Libby was involved in joint war planning and afterward in a joint defense board with Canada.

This memoir hits only the highlights of Admiral Libby's years as a junior officer, and is also less detailed about his concluding years of service than in discussing the World War II period. Throughout are sprinkled his opinions of the individuals with whom he served--men such as Richmond Kelly Turner, whom Admiral Libby found a good leader because he told his subordinates exactly what he wanted them to do.

Thanks are in order to Commander Etta-Belle Kitchen for conducting the interviews which are the basis of the oral history, to Ms. Susan Sweeney for the detailed index, and to Mrs. Deborah Reid of Techni-Type for the smooth-typed version of the transcript. Dr. John T. Mason, Jr., was director of the oral history program when the project was initiated, so it was done under his aegis.

                                                      Paul Stillwell
                                                      Director of Oral History
                                                      U.S. Naval Institute
                                                      December 1984

VICE ADMIRAL RUTHVEN E. LIBBY
UNITED STATES NAVY (RETIRED)

Ruthven Elmer Libby was born in Spokane, Washington, on December 22, 1900, son of the late Albion C. and Emma Lois (Chase) Libby. He attended Bryant Grammar School and North Central High School in Spokane, prior to his appointment to the U.S. Naval Academy, Annapolis, Maryland, from the Fifth District of his native state in July 1918. As a midshipman, he was a member of the Masqueraders and musical clubs and in 1920 was awarded the Maury Prize for Excellence in Physics. He was graduated with distinction and commissioned ensign on June 3, 1922, and subsequently progressed in rank, attaining that of rear admiral to date from October 1, 1947, having served in the temporary rank of commodore from April 23, 1945 until February 5, 1946. He was appointed to the rank of vice admiral, to date from February 3, 1956. On May 1, 1960 he was transferred to the Retired List of the U.S. Navy.

After graduation from the Naval Academy in June 1922, he sailed in the USS Chaumont to the Pacific Coast, and in August of that year joined the USS Tennessee, operating first with Division Eight, Battle Squadron Four, Pacific Fleet, and later with Division Five, Battleship Divisions, Battle Fleet. Detached from the Tennessee in November 1923, he returned to the East Coast, and in February 1924, reported for the course in naval construction at the Postgraduate School, Annapolis, Maryland. In September of that year he was assigned to the USS Utah, operating with Division Two, Scouting Fleet and in May 1926 transferred to the USS Colorado, also a unit of Division Five, Battle Fleet.

In June 1929 he returned to the Postgraduate School for instruction in electrical engineering, continuing the course at various places including Columbia University, New York, New York, from which he received the degree of Master of Science in 1931. On October 17, 1931 he was assigned duty in connection with the conversion of the USS Boggs, a radio-controlled light mobile target unit. He served as her engineering officer from her commissioning, December 19, 1931, until June 1934, during which time that destroyer was used in aerial bombing and surface gunnery practice in operation with Destroyers, Battle Force.

Following a two year assignment in the Electrical Design Section, Bureau of Engineering, Navy Department, Washington, D.C., he returned to sea in June 1936 as squadron engineer officer on the staff of Commander Destroyer Squadron Two. He was executive officer of the USS Macdonough, operating with Destroyers, Scouting Force, from February 1937 until May 1938, after which he served as engineer officer in the USS Northampton, flagship of Commander Cruiser Division Four, Scouting

Force. In July 1939 he returned to the Bureau of Engineering (consolidated with the Bureau of Construction and Repair and redesignated Bureau of Ships on June 24, 1940), and served in the Interior Communication Section of that bureau until November 23, 1940.

Reporting on December 11, 1940 as assistant naval attache, American Embassy, London, England, he served in that assignment until August 8, 1941, after which he had brief duty in the Office of the Chief of Naval Operations, Navy Department. On September 4, he joined the staff of the Commander in Chief, U.S. Atlantic Fleet. After the Japanese attack on Pearl Harbor, December 7, 1941, he transferred to the staff of the Commander in Chief, United States Fleet, for duty as aide. While in the latter assignment, he attended the conferences of the Combined Chiefs of Staff at London and Casablanca. He was awarded a Gold Star in lieu of a Fourth Legion of Merit for services as aide to the Commander in Chief, United States Fleet, from December 27, 1941 to March 22, 1943. The citation continues in part:

"Displaying sound judgment and outstanding ability, [he] proved of invaluable assistance to the Commander in Chief, United States Fleet, at the outset of the war. In his capacity as Aide, he provided necessary information and data which were essential to the Commander in Chief, United States Fleet, as a member of the Joint Chiefs of Staff, the Combined Chiefs of Staff, and at the great meeting of the Chiefs of Government of the Allied Powers at Casablanca. As Senior U.S. Naval Member of the Joint Staff Planning Committee from March 3 to October 10, 1945, he continued his outstanding service...exercising a nicety of judgment, and by exhibiting unusual knowledge, loyalty, perseverance and zeal, thereby contributing materially to the prosecution of the war."

In March 1943 he became Commander Destroyer Squadron One, USS Phelps, flagship, and with that squadron participated in the capture of Attu and the subsequent Aleutian Islands operations. When landings were made on the north coast of Attu his troops proceeded inland, and, in the bitter fighting which followed, furnished fire support for the troops. His squadron later participated in October 1943, in the Wake Island raid and capture of the Gilbert Islands.

For "exceptionally meritorious conduct...as Destroyer Squadron Commander during the seizure and occupation of enemy-held Attu Island in May 1943, and later of Kiska Island..." he was awarded the Legion of Merit. The citation continues:

"In command of a fire support unit, covering transports and initial landings in the Holtz Bay area, and later in complete control of patrolling vessel operations, [he] furnished an outstanding example of efficiency. Attacked on one occasion by enemy submarines he skillfully directed his destroyer squadron in the inflicting of damage on one undersea craft and the probable sinking of another, escaping with no damage to our forces."

On January 16, 1944 he assumed command of Destroyer Squadron 56, USS Newcomb, flagship, with additional duty as Commander Destroyer Division 111. Upon arrival at Pearl Harbor on February 27, he reported to Commander Destroyers, Pacific, for a month's temporary additional duty with the development of doctrine for shore bombardment by destroyers. With Squadron 56, he participated in the Marianas Campaign (capture and occupation of Saipan and Tinian), and the capture and occupation of the southern Palau Islands. For his contributions to these operations, he was awarded Gold Stars in lieu of the Second and Third Legion of Merit, each with Combat "V." The citations follow in part:

Gold Star in lieu of Second Legion of Merit: "For exceptionally meritorious conduct in the performance of outstanding services...as Commander of the Screen of Naval Attack Forces engaged in operations for the capture of enemy Japanese-held Saipan and Tinian Islands from June 15 to August 2, 1944. Exercising sound judgment and expert technical skill in drawing up plans for the protection of our forces and in directing those extremely difficult operations [he] prevented enemy submarines from penetrating the screen or damaging any of our vessels during the amphibious invasion of these strategic islands...[and] contributed in large measure to the final success of these vitally important operations."

Gold Star in lieu of Third Legion of Merit: "For...outstanding services as Commander of a Destroyer Squadron in the Pacific War Area from January 2 to June 14, 1944. Utilizing his wide experience and profound knowledge of destroyer operations [he] rendered inestimable service in creating and organizing Destroyer Bombardment Tactics, Destroyer Close-in Fire Support and Screening Operations. Constantly in the forward combat zones during this period, Captain Libby, by his sound judgment and complete mastery of the varied aspects of Naval warfare, directed his command in the successful fulfillment of numerous vital and hazardous missions in the area."

He is also entitled to the ribbon for and a facsimile of the Navy Unit Commendation awarded the USS Newcomb, flagship of Destroyer Squadron 56, for "outstanding heroism in action against enemy Japanese forces in the Saipan-Tinian operations, May 29 to August 5, 1944; Palau, September 6 to October 1, 1944; the Battle of Surigao Strait, October 24-25, 1944..."

Detached from command of Destroyer Squadron 56 on October 6, 1944, he was ordered to duty in the Planning Section of the Office of the Chief of Naval Operations, Navy Department. On March 28, 1945, he reported as Senior Naval Member of the Joint War Plans Committee, Joint Chiefs of Staff and served, in the rank of commodore, in that assignment until February 1946.

Following brief duty at Commander Cruiser Division 11, Pacific Fleet, before its dissolution, he assumed command on April 22, 1946 of the USS *Bremerton* at Shanghai, China. He was detached from command of that cruiser in February 1947, then joined the staff of the Commander in Chief, U.S. Pacific Fleet, as chief of staff for plans. After his promotion to rear admiral in November 1947, he was assigned to the Office of the Chief of Naval Operations, Navy Department, where on February 11, 1948 he became Deputy Chief, Strategic Plans. In October 1948 he reported as Director, General Planning Group, Naval Operations. He later had additional duty as a member of the Permanent Joint Board on Defense, United States-Canada. In September 1950 he returned to service afloat in command of Cruiser Division Three, commanding that division until March 1952. He served under Commander Naval Forces, Far East, participating as a United Nations Delegate at the Korean Truce Talks from November 1952 until late June 1953.

For outstanding services during the Korean conflict, he was awarded a Gold Star in lieu of the Fifth Legion of Merit with Combat "V," and an Oak Leaf Cluster in lieu of the Sixth Legion of Merit by the Department of the Army. The citations follow in part:

Gold Star in lieu of the Fifth Legion of Merit: "For distinguishing himself by exceptionally meritorious conduct...while serving in the dual capacity of Commander Cruiser Division Three and Commander Support Ships, Task Force 77. During the period from 18 April 1951 to 24 November 1951, while engaged in the Korean conflict, including actual combat, Rear Admiral Libby demonstrated outstanding initiative, aggressiveness and intelligence in the deployment and tactical control of the forces under his command. The highly accurate gunfire of his ships resulted in heavy enemy casualties and extensive damage to enemy installations and equipment, contributing materially to the overall war effect..."

Oak Leaf Cluster in lieu of the Sixth Legion of Merit: "For exceptionally meritorious conduct in the performance of outstanding services during the period from 26 November 1951 to 8 May 1952."

He was Assistant Chief of Naval Operations (Operations), Navy Department, from August 1952 until May 1954, after which he commanded the Battleship-Cruiser Force, U.S. Atlantic Fleet. In January 1956 he was assigned to the Office of the Chief of Naval Operations, and on May 1, that year, became Deputy Chief of Naval Operations (Fleet Operations and Readiness). On August 1, 1956 he was transferred to duty as Deputy Chief of Naval Operations (Plans and Policy) and in June 1958 reported as Commander First Fleet. He was serving in that assignment when relieved of all active duty pending his retirement, effective May 1, 1960.

In addition to the Legion of Merit with four Gold Stars and Oak Leaf Cluster (Army), and the Navy Unit of Commendation Ribbon, Vice

Admiral Libby has the Victory Medal (World War I); American Defense Service Medal, Base Clasp; Asiatic-Pacific Campaign Medal with silver star (five engagements); World War II Victory Medal; Navy Occupation Service Medal, Asia Clasp; China Service Medal; National Defense Service Medal; Korean Service Medal; and the United Nations Service Medal. He also has the Korean Presidential Unit Citation Badge and the Collar Order of Yun Hui awarded by the Government of China.

Vice Admiral Libby was married on May 8, 1926 to Miss Evelyn Maynard Claflin of New York, New York.

Authorization

The U.S. Naval Institute is hereby authorized to make available to libraries and other repositories of its choosing the transcripts of four oral history interviews concerning the life and career of the undersigned. The four interviews were recorded on 8 February 1970, 15 March 1970, 10 May 1970, and 7 June 1970 in collaboration with Commander Etta-Belle Kitchen, U.S. Navy (Retired), a representative of the Naval Institute.

The undersigned does hereby release and assign to the U.S. Naval Institute all right, title, restrictions, and interest in these four interviews. The copyright in both the oral and transcribed versions shall be the sole property of the U.S. Naval Institute. The tape recordings of the interviews are and will remain the property of the U.S. Naval Institute.

Signed and sealed this 14th day of December 1984

R.E. Libby
Vice Admiral, U.S. Navy (Retired)

Interview Number 1 with Vice Admiral Ruthven E. Libby, U.S. Navy (Retired)

Place: Admiral Libby's home in Coronado, California

Date: 8 February 1970

Subject: Admiral Chester W. Nimitz and Biography of Admiral Libby

Interviewer: Commander Etta-Belle Kitchen, U.S. Navy (Retired)

Q: My first series of questions is going to be concerning Admiral Libby's relationship with Admiral Nimitz, and I'd like to start out, Admiral, by just asking you to tell how well and over how long a period you did know the admiral.

Admiral Libby: Well, when I first knew Admiral Nimitz, it was at a great distance; he was a captain, and I was--oh, at the most, a lieutenant, I believe. He had command of the Rigel, which was the station ship here in San Diego, and I was the engineer officer of a destroyer. And then I knew him later on much more closely, of course, as I got a little further along in the Navy. He was Chief of the Bureau of Navigation for some time before the war. (It is now known as the Bureau of Personnel.) Right after Pearl Harbor, he was sent for by Admiral King and Secretary of the Navy Knox and sent out to take command of the Pacific Fleet at Pearl Harbor.* Thereafter, I encountered him from time to time during the war. The first time I met him directly, I believe, after Pearl Harbor, was out in San

---

*Secretary of the Navy Frank Knox.

Francisco. I was with Admiral Ernest J. King at the time.* Admiral King used to go out periodically to San Francisco and confer with Admiral Nimitz, that being sort of a convenient meeting point for both of them. Then, later on, when I went out to command a squadron of destroyers in the Pacific, he would come down to the dock to greet the ships whenever we came back from operations. First we went down to the Wake Island raid and then down to the Gilberts and Marianas and then finally to the Palaus. But every time we came back, anytime any ship came back to Pearl Harbor, whether it was a submarine or a destroyer or a cruiser or a battleship or whatever, Admiral Nimitz made a point of going down and meeting the ship. And that was the high spot of our lives, of course.

Q: Naturally. Do you have a recollection of any particular one that you could describe for me?

Admiral Libby: Well, I don't have any explicit recollection. I remember coming back after the--well, one operation, I don't remember a specific--I just remember Admiral Nimitz getting down to the dock to meet the ship when we tied up and, of course, he came aboard and he spoke to everybody. That was part of his regular technique of operation. Every man in the Pacific Fleet thought that Admiral Nimitz had a personal interest in him.

---

*Libby was then aide to Admiral King, who was Commander in Chief U.S. Fleet.

Libby #1 - 3

Q: I hadn't heard that before, that he met every ship.

Admiral Libby: Oh, yes, that was part of his wonderful personality. He was a busy man, you know. Ships came and went, and it took a lot of his time, but he never failed as far as that was concerned. He never missed once.

He never failed to have a very apropos story to fit any occasion. He was a horseshoe pitcher, and like Admiral King, he had an uncanny ability to pick men. He could pick the right man for the right job. But I never saw him ruffled; even when things were looking darkest, he never, never would give the slightest outward sign of concern. He was just calm and confident. A great leader, a wonderful person. He inspired confidence in everybody he dealt with. I never saw a larger turnout than up in San Francisco at his funeral. People came many miles, from all over the world. It was a remarkable tribute: a sign of the great admiration and respect people had for him. He was a wonderful person.

Q: But you didn't serve actually with him.

Admiral Libby: No, I never was on his staff, or I never was in a ship with him. I never served directly under Admiral Nimitz.

Q: Can you tell me something about the USS Rigel--where it was stationed and its purpose?

Libby #1 - 4

Admiral Libby: The Rigel was a station ship here in San Diego, stationed at the destroyer base, what is now called the naval station. I'm a little rusty, it may have been a destroyer tender, I think perhaps it was as well as being a station ship.*

Q: And did you say he had a baby living with him, too?

Admiral Libby: Oh, yes, I think it was their youngest daughter, the one who is now a nun, who lived aboard the Rigel with them. As I recall it, she was born while they were living aboard. I don't mean she was born in the ship, but she was born while they were living there.**

Q: What was your relationship with Admiral Nimitz at that point?

Admiral Libby: I was not serving under his command at all.

Q: Socially?

Admiral Libby: Oh well, we met them socially, of course, but I was not officially serving for him at that point.

Q: In '31 he went to the Rigel and stayed there for two years.

---

*USS Rigel (AD-13) was a destroyer tender.
**Mary Manson Nimitz, later to become a Roman Catholic nun, Sister Aquinas, was born 17 June 1931. She was the last of Admiral and Mrs. Nimitz's four children.

Libby #1 - 5

Admiral Libby: Yes, that's what it was. Then I was attached to the USS Boggs and spent most of our time at the destroyer base. It was a radio-controlled destroyer.

Q: I'm going to ask you about that in a minute. You spoke before we started taping of Admiral Nimitz's selection to go to Pearl. Do you know anything about that other than what was brought up?

Admiral Libby: When Pearl Harbor came, we were aboard the Augusta in Newport, which was Admiral King's flagship. He was Commander in Chief, U.S. Atlantic Fleet. And shortly thereafter he came aboard and told me to pack a bag; we were going down to Washington. It was sometime thereafter—things moved so fast—that Admiral King was made almost immediately Commander in Chief of the United States Fleet, and he and I were about the only people down there. The two of us were it for several days.

Q: Were you in the old Navy Building?

Admiral Libby: Yes, we were in the old Navy Building. They were the most decrepit looking offices you ever saw in your life. Along about that time, before Admiral King had even begun to assemble his staff as Commander in Chief of the U.S. Fleet, Admiral Nimitz was sent out to Pearl. As a matter of fact, I think that Secretary Knox and Admiral Nimitz went out together; I'm not sure.

Libby #1 - 6

Q: Did they?

Admiral Libby: I think so. I could be quite wrong about that. My recollection is that they went out together.*

Q: Now, I heard a story that he said that he wanted to go by train anonymously from Washington to the West Coast. Do you know anything about that?

Admiral Libby: I don't remember. It rings a bell, but only vaguely.

Q: Do you remember why he was selected--rather than somebody else?

Admiral Libby: Well, that I can't answer. I merely presume that he was regarded as the best man for the job.

Q: Did Admiral King have anything to do with the selection?

Admiral Libby: I think Admiral King had everything to do with it. I think. I'm guessing. I believe so. They probably could tell you. Have you looked up Admiral King's book? He probably mentions it in

---

*Actually, Secretary Knox left Washington on 9 December 1941 and flew out to Pearl Harbor to inspect the damage. Nimitz did not leave until 19 December. He took a train from Washington to the West Coast in the company of his aide, Lieutenant H. Arthur Lamar. Nimitz then flew from California to Hawaii on a PBY Catalina, arriving at Pearl Harbor on Christmas morning.

there, why Admiral Nimitz was selected.

Q: I'm trying to get something from you that might not be on the record yet.

Admiral Libby: I don't remember. Actually I don't know. I was not high enough up in the echelon to have been consulted, to be in on these consultations. I don't know.

Q: What was your grade then?

Admiral Libby: I was a lieutenant commander. No, Susie, when did I make commander? When I was over in England?

Mrs. Libby: No, right after--January of '42. You'd been selected sometime before.

Admiral Libby: That's right, I was lieutenant commander then. As I say, I don't remember specifically, but I can say this, that nobody around Washington was in the least surprised that Admiral Nimitz was sent out to take over, because he was highly regarded by everybody in the place. I mean civilians and military alike recognized him as a stand-out man.

Q: I have never heard anybody say anything about him that didn't make

Libby #1 - 8

him look almost perfect. It's hard to believe that a man in his position, which people are normally shooting at, somebody who is in that position, there's ...

Admiral Libby: Well, this is indicative of the man's character. You mentioned the fact that he never would write his memoirs, because he said he couldn't do it without hurting people, and he wasn't about to hurt people. Now some of his contemporaries in the other services--I mean the British, for instance, look at some of the British books. They don't care about hurting anybody.

Q: Well, some of our own, too, don't hesitate to put people in a bad light.

Admiral Libby: We weren't quite as bad as people like Alanbrooke who teed off at Eisenhower at every opportunity.* For that matter, some of the British used to tee off on Admiral King at every opportunity.

Q: When you went with Admiral King to any of the meetings with Admiral Nimitz in San Francisco, did you observe Admiral Nimitz at the time, and do you have any anecdotes or memoirs relating to him?

Admiral Libby: I went to only one of these meetings in San Francisco,

---

*Alan Francis Brooke (1st Viscount Alanbrooke), Chief of the Imperial General Staff, 1941-46, for Great Britain, known also for his antipathy toward General George C. Marshall.

but that particular one was quite memorable, because Admiral Nimitz had just gotten over a very bad bout of malaria which he had picked up on one of his visits to the Southwest Pacific or South Pacific. He wasn't feeling too hot, but it didn't affect his judgment in any way or his performance. I remember something came up about which he felt that Admiral King was unfairly criticizing one of his officers. He let Admiral King have it; he didn't take any guff from him. That is the only time I ever saw Admiral Nimitz come anywhere near losing his temper.

Q: Do you remember what he said?

Admiral Libby: I've forgotten what it was all about. Admiral King, of course, could be very blunt and could express himself very succinctly and very clearly, and Admiral Nimitz didn't like what he said about somebody. He thought he didn't have the right information. He straightened him out very quickly.

Q: How did Admiral Nimitz look when he got mad? I never heard anyone say that they saw Admiral Nimitz almost mad. I wonder how he looked and how he expressed it?

Admiral Libby: Well, he got a special glint in those eyes of his. You could tell, that's about the size of it. You can tell when a man is angry.

Libby #1 - 10

Q: General demeanor, of course.

Admiral Libby: And general appearance. This may not be--perhaps I was wrong in saying he was angry, but he was absolutely determined that Admiral King was not going to make an accusation against one of his people which he regarded as unfair.

Q: You have no recollection of who the person was?

Admiral Libby: I've forgotten. I don't know what it was all about.

Q: Do you remember any of the matters discussed at that time?

Admiral Libby: No, I don't. I would have to look it up. I don't remember. It was so long ago.

Q: Do you have papers and documents that you could refer to?

Admiral Libby: I don't have any of my own, but I could probably look back through the records and figure out when this was and what was being talked about. It was just--normally these meetings covered matters of immediate interest in the Pacific Ocean, matters in Admiral Nimitz's command, matters in General MacArthur's command, and matters which had been agreed to by the Combined Chiefs of Staff. It was just a review of the general progress of the war, the general strategic

Libby #1 - 11

situation, the general situation regarding allocation of shortages—who wasn't going to get what they had to have to fight the war. That sort of thing.

Q: You say, as many people have, that Admiral Nimitz was a story teller who always had the right story for the right situation. Do you recall any of his stories?

Admiral Libby: Not offhand.

Q: You're smiling as though maybe you do and don't want to tell it.

Admiral Libby: I would not like to attribute to the man something that perhaps he didn't say. I don't remember any specifically.

Q: Because everybody says that he had wonderful stories, and I've only had one man who remembered one, and he only remembers one.

Admiral Libby: The lovely part about some of his stories—he came from Texas, you know—was that he loved to deflate Texas. And some of his Texas stories effectively deflated Texans in a very nice way.

Q: I've heard that they were not necessarily stories for mixed company, some of them.

Libby #1 - 12

Admiral Libby: Oh, no, they were definitely not.

Q: Well, it's a shame you don't remember any. His biographer is trying to ...

Admiral Libby: Oh, they were not dirty; they were just sometimes a bit risque, you know.

Q: I think sometimes you can tell about a man from the stories he tells as much as by saying he won such-and-such a battle.

Admiral Libby: Well, he was a great raconteur; that goes without saying.

Q: Well, I'd be glad to add any other recollections you have of Admiral Nimitz, specific or general.

Admiral Libby: Well, they'd be pretty general, now. I know I was very happy indeed when, long after he had ceased to be Chief of Naval Operations--he never did retire, you know, being fleet admiral, you know, he didn't have to--but never bothered to retire. Several years after he had ceased to be CNO, he and his wife were living in an apartment in Berkeley without any help or anything else, and Rear Admiral E.E. Yeomans got smart and put him in Quarters One at Yerba

Buena.* Well, it made all the difference in the world in Admiral Nimitz's life. Once he got settled over there, and Catherine was there, and, of course, he had some help, stewards and whatnot, everybody who came to San Francisco made a point of going over to Treasure Island to see Admiral Nimitz, and the man just took a new lease on life, I thought. Well, it was wonderful, you see. He had a big house and he had plenty of servants, and he lived like an admiral ought to live. We're the only country in the world that doesn't look out for our senior retired people. In England, for instance, all the five-star generals, the big shots are lords, or something or other, and they give them great big estates, and they give them a tremendous amount of this, that, and the other, but we don't do that for our people. On the other hand, we do better by our lesser lights. I mean anyone who doesn't get right up to the top in the British armed services, practically starves to death when they retire; they get almost nothing. Unless you hit the top rung, you're out of luck when you retire.

Q: That's kind of true of the English economy all through.

Admiral Libby: But it was really very fine for Admiral Nimitz and

---

*In the summer of 1963, Commander Western Sea Frontier was detached without relief, so his duties were assumed by the Commandant 12th Naval District, Rear Admiral Elmer E. Yeomans, USN. Having one admiral performing the duties previously held by two left Quarters One vacant, and Admiral and Mrs. Nimitz moved to Yerba Buena in late July 1963. Admiral Nimitz also had an office in the Western Sea Frontier headquarters on the adjoining Treasure Island.

Libby #1 - 14

Mrs. Nimitz too, in the latter part of Admiral Nimitz's life, to have the proper setup so that he could really see people. People would hesitate to go see him when he and Catherine were living in the apartment, because, you know, they thought it might be an imposition.

Q: Was it an apartment? I thought it was a house.

Admiral Libby: I thought it was an apartment. I don't know. I never did go there. I could be wrong. It was not as adequate as it should have been.

Q: I think they did not have help even.

Admiral Libby: I don't believe they did, no.

Q: So I'm glad that he got what we feel is due him, even though it was in his latter years.

Admiral Libby: That's right. Of course, I felt badly after he died, that they didn't let her stay in that house. They should have. But, of course, they didn't, the law being what it was. But I can say this about Admiral Nimitz, that I think most everybody will share--my recollections of him are very happy ones. He was a very happy sort of person. He was fun to be with and fun to be around, and he certainly knew his job.

Libby #1 - 15

Q: To grasp all the details he had to do is beyond my comprehension of a mentality.

Admiral Libby: Well, he had quite a remarkable psychology, I think. Now here's an example, for whatever it's worth. As the war moved on out into the Pacific, as the Japanese started to get more and more on the run, Admiral Nimitz could perfectly well have stayed snug as a bug in a rug there at Makalapa in very pleasant surroundings, but he didn't do that.* He proceeded to go out to Guam and work under far less physically comfortable circumstances and in a far less salubrious climate, because he felt that being out there he was closer to the scene of action and closer to things going on and he might get some information a little bit quicker.

Q: Did you ever visit those quarters on Guam?

Admiral Libby: Oh, yes, I've been there. I was only in them once, I believe, when he was there. I spent quite a lot of time on Guam after the war. They were adequate. The quarters they had on Guam were very nice, delightful, except it was hotter than a firecracker on Guam. Always. Miserable climate. I don't like hot, damp weather. The working facilities were nothing compared to what he had in Pearl.

---

*Makalapa was the location of Admiral Nimitz's quarters on Oahu, near Pearl Harbor, before he moved to Guam in early 1945.

Libby #1 - 16

Q: Can you expand a little bit?

Admiral Libby: Well, I mean, he had a tremendous, really a fine setup there at Pearl, you know with all his type commanders around, handy, and this, that, and the other. The quarters in Guam were put up during the war, of course. They were--well, they kept the rain out, and they had enough room, but there was certainly nothing fancy about them. They were rather primitive. I imagine that the staff found it more difficult to function there. I don't know. I wasn't on the staff, of course. My impression was that while the headquarters there were sufficient for the day, they were certainly in no way luxurious and in no way more than adequate.

Q: He went back to the CNO right at the end of 1945. Let's see, I can tell you specifically--November 26 for a term of two years. He was confirmed by the Senate. He left the Pacific very soon after Tokyo.

Admiral Libby: The war was over. He relieved Admiral King in '45.

Q: On December 5, 1945 he relieved Fleet Admiral Ernest J. King as Chief of Naval Operations.

Admiral Libby: Something came up, some international crisis or something or other came up shortly thereafter. When was the Berlin

Libby #1 - 17

blockade? '46? '48? I don't know. Anyway, something, somebody wanted Admiral Nimitz to go somewhere, go on a junket which would have been a very pleasant outing, a very pleasant trip, but he wouldn't go, because he just didn't want to leave his command post, he said. I remember he told me that, but I've forgotten what it's all about. He just didn't want to get away from his job.

Q: He left almost at the same time you came. He had gone from CNO at the time you had duty there.

Admiral Libby: I guess so, yes.

Mrs. Libby: Yes, because we didn't get back from Honolulu until February of '48, remember?

Admiral Libby: That's right.

Q: And he left at the end of '47, as I recall.

Admiral Libby: Yes, Admiral Denfeld relieved him, I believe.*

Q: Correct.

---

*Admiral Louis E. Denfeld, USN, relieved Admiral Nimitz as Chief of Naval Operations on 15 December 1947.

Libby #1 - 18

Admiral Libby: That's right. I went out to Pearl with Admiral Denfeld, and then I came back with him—or shortly after he took over, that's right.

Q: Did you say that you were on a ship coming into Pearl when Admiral Nimitz did come down and welcome the men back?

Admiral Libby: Oh, yes, indeed.

Q: Do you have any recollection of how he looked or what he said at that time?

Admiral Libby: Oh, he looked fine. He always looked fine, you know. He had an open khaki shirt and was very tanned, and fine looking.

Q: I wonder if you remember what Admiral Nimitz said on that day. Would you possibly remember?

Admiral Libby: Oh, I don't know. I couldn't begin to remember specifically what he said. He gave all of us the impression that we personally had won the war, I remember that.

Q: Well, I'm sure you did. I'm sure you did.
Well, we might leave Admiral Nimitz for the time being and start with you.

Libby #1 - 19

Admiral Libby: From the sublime to the ridiculous.

Q: I wouldn't say that. I would say "from the sublime to the sublime." Well, your career is certainly a distinguished one, so if we might start on that, would you be agreeable?

Admiral Libby: Oh, we might as well get it over with. It won't take very long.

Q: Well, you may be surprised. In the first place my biography says that you were born in 1920 and that you graduated from the Naval Academy in 1922.

Admiral Libby: A typographical error. I was born in 1900. I was born in Spokane, Washington, December 22, 1900.

Q: Almost a Christmas present, weren't you? Yes, I knew you came from Spokane, and I guess you're typical of many fine naval officers who went to the Naval Academy and never had had before any association with Navy or ...

Admiral Libby: That's right.

Q: Why did you choose the Academy?

Libby #1 - 20

Admiral Libby: Well, I read a couple of books about the Naval Academy and a couple of books about the Navy, and I was very anxious to go, so my father managed to dredge me up, I believe, a third alternate appointment, and I went.

Q: Where did you get the books on the Navy? At school?

Admiral Libby: No, somebody gave me one once and then I bought a couple. I don't know. I just bought them in a bookstore.

Q: Do you have any relatives that were Navy?

Admiral Libby: No, no. There's a namesake, Commander Miles A. Libbey, who spells his name with an "E," but he was no relation to me. I have no relatives in the Navy at all.

Q: Well, again, what you say about being a third alternative--as you are well aware, it has happened in the case of some of our finest people--that they were not the first choice of the district or of the time and turned out to be wonderful, fine naval officers.

Mrs. Libby: Don't forget that your father would not let you go the year you graduated from high school, though. Your father would not let you go until you were 17.

Libby #1 - 21

Admiral Libby: What's that got to do with it?

Q: That's interesting.

Mrs. Libby: No, he graduated from high school when he was 16, and his father wouldn't let him go to the Naval Academy until he was 17.

Admiral Libby: I don't know whether it was a question of not letting me go, or whether we couldn't get an appointment until then. I don't remember specifically. Representative Clarence C. Dill gave me one eventually.

Q: Oh, yes, I remember him.

Admiral Libby: Afterwards was a senator and then after two terms in the Senate he turned in his suit and voluntarily stepped down. He got fed up with Washington. He just couldn't take it any longer.

Q: I didn't know that, but I did know the name of Senator Dill. I'm from Oregon, so I knew the name.

Admiral Libby: He's still alive. He's living up in Spokane. I get a card from him occasionally.

Q: Tell me about your activities while you were a midshipman.

Libby #1 - 22

Admiral Libby: Well, I didn't do much. I wasn't an athlete. My only extracurricular activities were the stage gang and the Masqueraders. I was on the electrical side of that, made electric signs and this, that, and the other.

Q: Did you ever play a part in any of their productions?

Admiral Libby: No, I was not handsome enough to be a man and I was not the right ...

Q: Contours?

Admiral Libby: Contours to be in a--no, I was never an actor.

Q: I know they put on a lot of memorable productions.

Admiral Libby: We had a lot of fun. My Naval Academy career was singularly undistinguished.

Q: Well, contrary to what you say, I think you're being too modest, because the record says that you graduated with distinction.

Admiral Libby: Well, that just means that I had a high class standing.

Libby #1 - 23

Q: Where did you stand in your class?

Admiral Libby: I graduated third in the class.

Q: That's certainly noteworthy.

Admiral Libby: A lot of people do it.

Q: Only one each year. And didn't you excel in physics?

Admiral Libby: I got the pair of binoculars from the Maury Prize as a youngster, given by some of the southern ladies, daughters of the Confederacy or something, for excellence in physics. I stood one in my class in the physics course that particular one.

Q: That's probably why you were able to go ahead and get your master's degree later on.

Admiral Libby: Well, that's the postgraduate instruction. Everybody gets his master's at PG School.

Q: Tell me, do you have any other recollections of your time at the Academy?

Admiral Libby: Oh, a great many recollections, but none of them were

Libby #1 - 24

of any importance. I mean you can't live in a place for four years and not have recollections of it.

Q: Right. But are there any things that happened that you think are unique, that, say, only you know, that would be of interest to someone reading a history?

Admiral Libby: I wouldn't think so, no.

Q: How many were in the Academy at that time? How many in your class?

Admiral Libby: We started off with, let me see, nine hundred and—just under 1,000—about 980. We graduated 541 four years later.*

Q: That's pretty high attrition, isn't it?

Admiral Libby: That's normal. Forty percent is normal. During my time, that was the normal attrition. About 40% of the people that entered didn't graduate for one reason or another. And of the 541 who were graduated, we commissioned only about 360. It was right after World War I, and peace was the order of the day, and we

---

*The Naval Academy Alumni Register shows that the class of 1922 had 539 graduates and 359 non-graduates, which computes to an attrition rate of 39.98%.

had the disarmament naval conference and all that kind of baloney. And it could be proved mathematically, and was before I graduated, that no one in the class of '22 would ever rise beyond the rank of lieutenant commander, because they'd be too old, you see, promotion being what it was. So a great many of my class resigned on graduation with the blessing of the authorities--rather urged to do so. They wanted to get rid of them, because they didn't see anything. By the time 1922 came around, you see, there was a glut on the market among ensigns. So, a large number of my class resigned on graduation.

Q: That would be the group that weren't commissioned?

Admiral Libby: That's right. All of us that were commissioned, of course, didn't resign.

Q: And much psychological comment about if you don't, you're never going to get anywhere anyway?

Admiral Libby: No, they didn't say--that was never official, but that was an understanding. There was a considerable amount of soul-searching by all of us as to whether we would stick around and take a commission and take a chance, or whether we would get out and get into civilian life. And those who decided to get out did so.

Q: Why did you stay?

Libby #1 - 26

Admiral Libby: Well, I wanted to be a naval officer, primarily. I enjoyed it. I thought I'd just take a chance. Maybe it was just a lack of initiative, I don't know.

Q: I would think not.

Admiral Libby: I wanted to be in the Navy.

Q: Because you were one of the ones that did the soul-searching, I'm sure.

Admiral Libby: Oh yes, yes. We all did. As much soul-searching as a kid that age would do.

Q: How much soul-searching can you do at 22?

Admiral Libby: Right.

Q: What did your father do?

Admiral Libby: He was a court reporter. He was born in Limerick, Maine, in the year of our Lord 1848, and believe me in Limerick, Maine, in 1848, only the tough survived, as he used to say. Then he went on out to Osage, Iowa, where he married my mother, and then he proceeded from there to Spokane Falls, Washington Territory, where he

Libby #1 - 27

arrived in 1888. The next year the town burned down. But his court sat up in Wallace, Idaho, which he decided was not a suitable place for his family, so he left us and parked us in Spokane, and he would go up there--Wallace, Idaho, is 60 miles from Spokane, and you can get there now, of course, in about 40 minutes. In those days the only way to get there was on the rather dubious interurban electric train. The roads were impassable or nonexistent. He would just go up there and stay for the whole term of court, and he would be gone for months at a time.

Q: Did he take shorthand?

Admiral Libby: Oh yes, he was excellent at shorthand; he was a Gregg man.

Q: I wonder where he learned it.

Admiral Libby: That I don't know.

Q: This really has nothing to do with your biography, except I think it's interesting. You're the first person I've interviewed whose father happened to come from that line, and I have had experience with it, and I know it takes a very high degree of skill, so I can to some extent understand your clarity of mind.

Libby #1 - 28

Admiral Libby: He was an excellent shorthand man, an excellent reporter. Of course, he had some of his own shortcuts, as they all do. But he was not the best businessman in the world. When he first came out to Spokane, he was in the real estate business, but he promptly lost his shirt. And, of course, he was up in Wallace at the height of all the big mining discoveries being made up there, you know, the Bunker Hill and Sullivan and the Anaconda and all the silver, lead, and whatnot mines. And when he died at the age of 88, someone went up in the attic and found a trunk full of mining stock. None of it was any good. You'd think by the shotgun approach he would have hit at least one. He was not a financial genius.

Q: I know lawyers are rarely financial geniuses. My father was a lawyer. But I can understand something of your intellect as I see your background from here.

Can you tell me something of your first duties?

Admiral Libby: I graduated and went to the USS Tennessee. Then I decided I wanted to be a naval constructor. I went back to postgraduate school in '23. And, of course, the transportation facilities being what they were and the Navy not having any money, we didn't get back to the Naval Academy until about February. And we had a compressed course, short course. The more I saw of it, the more I decided I did not want to be a naval constructor, so I requested to go back to sea duty and was allowed to go back to sea duty.

Q: I was wondering about that, because it's obvious that you went from the fleet to constructor school and then back to the fleet again.

Admiral Libby: The naval constructors were very irate, and it was widely and freely prophesied that I would come to no good end by going back to the fleet, but I managed to go back to the fleet, aided and abetted by Admiral Wilson, who was Superintendent of the Naval Academy at the time.* He gave me moral encouragement.

Q: Why didn't you like naval construction?

Admiral Libby: Oh, I wanted to be a naval officer, that's all. I didn't want to be a naval architect. They never go to sea, but what really threw me, what really was the last straw--I went up to the David Taylor Model Basin, along with the rest of the class. Here was this captain in the Construction Corps, happy as a clam at high tide, riding back and forth on the model basin towing carriage.

Q: Carriage?

Admiral Libby: On the carriage in the model basin, towing a model and watching the graphs and just enjoying himself to no end. I decided that that was not the life for me. I just decided I didn't want to do

---

*Rear Admiral Henry B. Wilson, USN, Superintendent of the Naval Academy from 1921 to 1925.

Libby #1 - 30

that.

Q: That didn't look like a naval officer's career.

Admiral Libby: Well, they do wonderful work. It's a marvelous profession, but I decided it was not for me, so I went back to sea.

Q: Weren't you lucky to be able to make your choice at that time?

Admiral Libby: Quite fortunate and, as I say, the naval constructors were very, very irate. They didn't like it.

Mrs. Libby: You weren't supposed to amount to a hill of beans.

Admiral Libby: Oh, I was finished as far as they were concerned. Captain George Rock—I believe he was, senior naval constructor—he wrote a letter which, of course, became part of my official record, and I saw it several years later, and it amused me highly.*

Q: What did it say?

Admiral Libby: Oh, it just took a dim view of my having wasted the government's time and money by starting to be a naval constructor and

---

*Captain George H. Rock, Construction Corps, USN, Assistant to the Chief of the Bureau of Construction and Repair.

then deciding I didn't want to, you know.

Q: Had that been put in your record without your knowledge?

Admiral Libby: Oh, no.

Q: You got a copy of it?

Admiral Libby: No, I didn't get a copy of it, but I knew it had been. I saw it. I knew it was going in there. Oh, no. Nothing underhanded about it. I think what it was actually, was an endorsement on my request to go back to sea. Then I went to the Utah and I was on board the Utah for a couple of years, and then I got married to my present wife on the ninth of May, 1926.

Mrs. Libby: Eighth.

Admiral Libby: Eighth of May, 1926. The ninth of March is her birthday, and the eighth of May. I was ordered out to the Colorado, so I left the Utah after three years.

Q: What were your duties on the Utah and the Colorado?

Admiral Libby: I was turret officer on the Utah—first, assistant turret officer then turret officer, turret four. I had the fourth

Libby #1 - 32

division. When I went back out to the Colorado, I had the plotting room and then I became spot one, in gunnery.

Q: Where were you living then?

Admiral Libby: We lived in San Pedro. We lived--well, let's see. Susie got very ill shortly after we got out there. She went up to this hospital in Tacoma. We went up for the summer, and this gal took care of her. But we lived in all these little holes in the wall in San Pedro, small places where ensigns and lieutenants (junior grade) lived.

Mrs. Libby: 3806-1/2.

Admiral Libby: Oh, that was a lush place. 3806-1/2 South Pacific, that was a really lush flat. We just lived, you know, in rented houses, rented furnished houses.

Q: All your classmates were doing the same thing?

Admiral Libby: Oh, sure. We had a lot of fun. The Navy in those days was quite a different animal from what it is now, you know. Much smaller, and we had almost no fuel oil, so we never went to sea very much, and we didn't have any money for bullets, so we fired the guns once in a great while. We had about four or five standard gunnery practices in which we would actually shoot, and the rest of the time we just drilled. And we'd get under way in the morning and come in in the afternoon, generally. Sometimes we'd stay out two or three whole days at a time. We'd go off on the fleet problem every year, which would take about three months. We'd go to Panama or sometimes ...

Q: And you knew everybody?

Admiral Libby: Oh, knew everybody, sure. You knew all the admirals and--when I was graduated there was 6,212 officers in the United States Navy--total. That included the dentists and the doctors and everybody else. Of course, everybody knew all the admirals--only a handful of them--and you knew most of the captains. At least you knew who they were. Nowadays, good Lord.

Q: Well, and you had actually gone to school with a lot of them because when you were--your first year you knew the three ahead of you, and when you were the top you knew the three behind you, so you had gone to school with a big portion of them.

Admiral Libby: Well, let's see, where were we? We were aboard the Colorado. And I went back to take a postgraduate course in electrical engineering.

Q: What prompted you to do that?

Libby #1 - 34

Admiral Libby: Well, I was at the stage in life where you had to get a PG course. It was sort of expected of you, you know, sort of required reading.

Q: And you had that kind of mind, didn't you, that you wanted to improve yourself?

Admiral Libby: Not particularly, but it was a good idea. Seemed to be a good idea at the time. We had a year at Annapolis and a year at New York, Columbia, and then I went from there to this radio-controlled destroyer which ...

Q: Let's not skip over, though, that you got your master's degree at Columbia. In 1931.

Admiral Libby: That's right, I guess it was. Was it '31? '31, yes. Then I put in three horrible years in the Boggs, '31 to '34, and from there I ...

Q: Could we talk a minute about the Boggs and why it was so horrible?

Admiral Libby: Well, there were only three officers in the ship, and the exec and I had the duty every other day. And I had a total engineering force of 23 men, and I had to operate a regular standard destroyer engineering plant which, in addition, was supposed to run by itself. We'd abandon the ship, you see, then it would run around in the ocean, and the captain would control it by radio.

Q: Is that what it means when it says radio-controlled light mobile target unit?

Admiral Libby: That's right. It was a four-pipe destroyer. Regular old four-stacker destroyer. We put some radio gear in it, and it was supposed to be used as a target. The first time we actually used it as a target the aviators shot it up, filled it full of holes, so after that they decided it would be smart to have it tow a target. They could shoot at the target instead of the ship.

Q: That makes sense. What did you do? You were down at the destroyer base.

Admiral Libby: Yes, we'd just take it out to sea, and then everybody would get off the ship, and then we would go over to another destroyer that had the control teletype keyboard, and the captain would control it from there.

Q: You didn't do the controlling?

Admiral Libby: Oh, no. The skipper did. First, we had Boyd Rufus Alexander for two years and then John Emerson Williams for a year, and

Libby #1 - 36

it was just an awful lot of work.* I mean, let's say lifting a turbine between Saturday noon and Monday morning, you see, with 23 men and all that kind of thing. Hard labor, and it got a little monotonous having duty every other day. And when we were at sea, the exec and I would stand six hours on and six hours off, watches. And that got a little tiresome after a while.

Q: How often did you go to sea?

Admiral Libby: Not very often. Not too often. We went off on a couple of fleet problems, and we would go up to Mare Island. I don't know, we weren't at sea very much—any extended period. These operations for target shooting, we'd go out about maybe two or three days at a crack, but that was not ...

Mrs. Libby: You mentioned the captain's tires?

Admiral Libby: Boyd Rufus Alexander was absolutely certain that the ship was agile enough so the aviators couldn't hit it, you see. Couldn't hit it with bombs. He'd just bought four new automobile tires, and for some reason they were still in the squadron commander's cabin on the forecastle of the destroyer. And we went out for one of these shoots, and the aviators proceeded to throw bombs at it. I don't believe they hit it with the bombs. Then they proceeded

---
*Both Alexander and Williams held the rank of lieutenant commander while in command of the USS _Boggs_.

to strafe it with machine guns, and in the course of strafing it with .50-caliber machine guns they managed to trip the ship out so she stopped, and they made dive-bombing runs on it with their machine guns and just riddled the captain's tires with machine gun bullets. The captain was annoyed.

Q: I'm sure that he was more than somewhat annoyed. Was this the only ship of its kind?

Admiral Libby: No, we had two. We had the Boggs and the Stoddert. The Stoddert was the first one, and the Boggs was number two.* They were a little different plants, but they were the same general idea.

Q: Was anything accomplished with it?

Admiral Libby: A waste of time and money. Later on, they took the old Utah, the erstwhile battleship, Utah, and made a radio-controlled ship out of her, too. What they ever did with it, I don't know. It was an idea that somebody had that, like a lot of these ideas, was not too successful.

Q: What had they thought to accomplish with it?

---

*These ships comprised Mobile Target Division One. In 1933, the Stoddert was replaced by the USS Lamberton.

Admiral Libby: Just to have a target that you could shoot at, you see. Give a degree of realism to gunnery exercises. Just as we have targets now, you know, for the jet pilots and whatnot--Ryan's Aerobee drones and all that kind of stuff.* It's very difficult to practice gunnery unless you have a proper target, you see. And this was supposed to give a high-speed target people could shoot at.

Q: Was this somebody's idea that this would be better than what they had been doing before?

Admiral Libby: Well, it was a new idea. I just don't think it was a very fruitful one. The fact that it's been abandoned would indicate that. I don't even believe that it served a good purpose at the time. It may have, but I never felt that it was a very great accomplishment. Then I went back to Washington, for duty in the Bureau of Engineering--'34 to '36. Then I came out as engineer officer of Destroyer Squadron Two, I believe. Captain Poteet was the squadron commander, in '36.** And then we folded up the squadron, and I went over to become exec of the Macdonough, which was a brand-new "gold-plated" destroyer, one of the 1,500-tonners.

Q: And did you enjoy that?

---
*Ryan makes a number of remotely piloted drone aircraft used for target practice.
**Captain Fred H. Poteet, USN.

Libby #1 - 39

Admiral Libby: Very much, indeed. It was wonderful. A brand, spanking new destroyer, you know, the finest in the fleet. I reported aboard one morning; we got under way at noon and started off in a generally southwesterly direction. "Count" Grassie, who lives here, was the skipper.* I was the new exec, you know, all proud of myself, been riding the four-pipe destroyers for years, and nothing had ever bothered me. And we got outside the sea buoy, and 20 minutes later the new exec was just as seasick as a goat.

Q: Was that the first time you'd ever been seasick?

Admiral Libby: First time I'd ever been. These 1,500-tonners were just as tight--very stiff, you see. Just like riding the string on a violin. They would flip over in nothing flat. They had a period of roll of four seconds, which was from vertical to this way and back-- four seconds.

Q: Four seconds for the total roll?

Admiral Libby: That's right. Complete cycle. As I say, in about 20 minutes the new exec was just as seasick as he could possibly be.

Q: And can you tell me about where the Macdonough operated and some of the experiences you had aboard her?

---
*Lieutenant Commander Herbert J. Grassie, USN.

Libby #1 - 40

Admiral Libby: We operated out of San Diego here. Then the most memorable thing we did there, as I recall it, was the fleet problem we went on. We left here and went up to Bremerton to join up with the New Mexico and the Concord. There was another destroyer along with us. It was the Aylwin, another 1,500-tonner. We were to represent a task force which had gone on up or had been shot up in an engagement and had gone on into Dutch Harbor, which is up in the Aleutian Islands, for battle repairs. And that was what we were supposed to represent. So we started from here to Bremerton, and we had absolutely foul weather all the way up the coast. Just foul as could be. We got into Bremerton in due course, and then we left with the New Mexico and Concord and headed out through the Strait of Juan de Fuca, and we were bringing up the rear of the column. The New Mexico led the column and then the Concord and then us and then the other destroyer. Anyway, the minute we stuck our nose outside the strait, here came the biggest roller I've ever seen in my life. It was just from horizon to horizon on either side of the strait. It was a big, huge thing. The New Mexico hit it, and she threw spray all over the place. She just hit it like a rock. We found out afterwards that it had broached over the forecastle and knocked several men down and broke a man's leg, wiped him against the turret. Then the Concord hit it. She didn't do much better. Then it was our turn. We were all sort of holding our breath. We just rode up one side, sailed over the top, and down the other side, without shipping a drop of water. Then we proceeded on course 287, which is the course from our point of departure from the strait to Dutch Harbor. This big storm out in the mid-Pacific, which is what made it so bad weather all the way up, produced a tremendous groundswell. We rolled 57 degrees for two solid weeks. We were only making about eight knots. We had to kill the time so as not to get up there too soon.

Q: It must have been just ghastly.

Admiral Libby: Oh, it really was something. And we tried to get Wally Vernou, who was the admiral in charge, to change course a little bit, but Wally wouldn't do it.* They were doing all right.

Q: How far could that ship roll and still stay?

Admiral Libby: It could roll 57 degrees without overturning, because it did.

Q: But you wouldn't think so.

Admiral Libby: They were pretty stable. That's one thing that made them so stiff, you see. They had very little topside weight. We didn't have any antiaircraft guns. They loaded them down during the war so that slowed the roll period down a bit and made them much more

---

*Rear Admiral Walter N. Vernou, USN, Commander Cruisers Battle Force, embarked in the Concord.

Libby #1 - 42

comfortable. Then after wandering around up there for—it's taken two weeks to get up there, spending three or four days up there with the williwaws blowing and having a hell of a time keeping our hook down. We free-ballooned all over Dutch Harbor. Finally, one night we got permission to get under way and get out to sea because we just couldn't keep the hook down with the williwaws blowing. Do you know what a williwaw is?

Q: Yes, but explain it further.

Admiral Libby: Well, a williwaw is a peculiar wind which they have up in the Aleutian Islands in the wintertime, and you'll have an absolutely flat calm, and then you will have a 60-knot wind blowing, say, from due north. It will blow four or five minutes, and then another flat calm and then you'll have another gale of 60-70 knots blow from the southeast or the southwest or an entirely different point of the compass. And this happens about every five minutes, and with those destroyers, they had a high forecastle, only one light anchor down, and after a couple of minutes of this williwaw, you'd sort of get straightened out and more or less headed into the wind, and then the next thing it'd hit you broadside on, and you find you'd dragged your anchor all over. You couldn't get your hook to hold at all. So after a couple of days of fighting this, we decided to hell with it and we got permission to go to sea, and we steamed around the Bering Sea for two or three days and got back in just in time to witness one of the most notable occurrences that took place up there and I don't know whether this is proper for recorded history or not, but it's true.

Q: Of course it is.

Admiral Libby: The Concord had to go alongside the New Mexico to fuel. The assistant engineer officer of the New Mexico was one Hyman G. Rickover, who was ...

Q: Oh, really?

Admiral Libby: ... a lieutenant, and the assistant engineer officer of the Concord was Angus Sinclair.* So here you had a Scotchman and a gentleman of Rickover's persuasion. I forgot to say that the New Mexico was fighting for the engineering E efficiency award among the battleships, and the Concord was fighting for the engineering efficiency award among the cruisers. Each of these two gentlemen was convinced that the other was out to gyp him, you see, that the New Mexico would charge the Concord for more oil than they got, or that the Concord would get more oil than they were charged for. As I say, with the williwaws blowing and whatnot, although the New Mexico had gone in some tiny little cove up there and was reasonably sheltered,

---

*Lieutenant Hyman G. Rickover, USN, who became famous years later as the head of the Navy's nuclear power program; Lieutenant George Angus Sinclair, USN.

nobody was too happy with these two ships alongside each other in this kind of weather. But Admiral Rickover sounded his tanks and re-sounded his tanks until he was absolutely sure that he had every drop of oil accounted for before the fueling started. He had to know exactly how much he had before he started giving some to the Concord. And after what seemed an interminable delay, he finally gave the word to go ahead and start fueling the Concord, and somebody below started to pump. And the oil hose was up on the boat deck and it hadn't been quite hooked up yet, and the plug blew out and covered the executive officer with a solid stream of oil. In those days, we had nothing but blue uniforms; we didn't have any proper war clothes. The exec had on his number one blue overcoat and his nice hat and stuff, you know--here this 8-inch stream of oil hit the quarterdeck of the New Mexico, brilliant, shiny teak planks, you know. Well, it didn't do the exec any good, and it didn't do the quarterdeck of the New Mexico any good, but the deluge was shut off eventually.

Q: What was the language at the time?

Admiral Libby: Well, they just opened the wrong valve.

Q: I say what was their language, though, when this happened?

Admiral Libby: I wasn't there. I don't know.

Libby #1 - 45

Q: I can imagine.

Admiral Libby: But I do know that Admiral Rickover took steps instantly, and he plugged up all the scuppers so that the oil didn't run overboard, and he had his men out with dustpans and buckets to gather up the oil that had leaked out and pour it back down into the manhole again. He lost a minimum amount of oil.

Q: That's a good story, isn't it?

Admiral Libby: It's true.

Q: I'm sure it is, and it's very good.

Admiral Libby: Oh, my. Well, then after we left there we went boiling out. The fleet problem called for us to leave Dutch Harbor, then proceed south toward Honolulu at 25 knots. Well, of course, in those days, to travel at 25 knots would be just like flying. Good Lord. Or 21 knots. The New Mexico couldn't make 25 knots. Anyway, we went down at top speed, arrived just in time for the big battle that we were supposed to take part in. We were ruled out of action in 20 minutes by the umpire's decision, after all this travel.

Q: What sank you?

Libby #1 - 46

Admiral Libby: I don't know what sank us; something did.

Q: Well, this experience up in Dutch Harbor was almost a forecast of later days for you, wasn't it?

Admiral Libby: It was very interesting, and we were made quite well aware with that cruise that life was not all beer and skittles. That was the first time any of us had been up in that part of the world, and it was a tough experience.

Q: That was your big job up 'til now, as exec. Didn't you enjoy that duty?

Admiral Libby: Wonderful. I enjoyed it thoroughly. Second in command and you take and you sort of run the ship and see that everything is done and administered and whatnot.

Q: Did you give me the name of the skipper?

Admiral Libby: Herbert J. Grassie. And Ed Kidder relieved him.* Grassie was in the Macdonough for two years. And Ed Kidder relieved him. Ed Kidder is dead now.

Q: Did you have any other operations that were ...

---
*Lieutenant Commander Edmund J. Kidder, USN.

Libby #1 - 47

Admiral Libby: Oh, yes. Normal, routine. We had torpedo practices, gunnery practices and all that sort of thing.

Q: But not as outstanding.

Admiral Libby: But that's the one I remember best on that ship.

Q: And then you went over to another ship.

Admiral Libby: Engineer officer of the Northampton, yes.

Q: Now, why did you go from exec to engineering officer?

Admiral Libby: Well, I got promoted to lieutenant commander ...

Q: I see.

Admiral Libby: ... and too senior to be exec, and besides, someone else wanted the job, and they needed an engineer officer on the Northampton, so I was ordered up there. Two items come to mind, one trivial and one of some importance. The Northampton-class ships were big and comfortable but with little firepower and less ability to stay afloat. I used to say that I could have come in at night with my 1,500-tonner and sunk the Northampton with a single torpedo. And, sure enough, she took two Jap torpedoes during the war and sank like a stone.*

On most ships the first lieutenant and the chief engineer are mortal enemies, since the first one has to keep the ship clean, and the latter dirties it up. In the Northampton this was not the case. The first lieutenant, Jerry O'Donnell, and I were classmates and fast friends.** Our single mortal enemy was the supply officer, one of those old-line types, all too prevalent in the prewar Navy, who felt that his mission in life was to study the Supplies and Accounts Manual exhaustively so that he could find a reason for saying that anything you needed to run your department you couldn't have. And I mean anything. Jerry and I used to take him to the executive officer every now and again, and the exec would tell him to get us what we had to have, or else. This was a damned nuisance. I cite this matter because it bears directly on one thing Admiral King did almost immediately on becoming CominCh. He sent for a commander in the Supply Corps, whose name was Young, promoted him to rear admiral, made him Chief of the Bureau of Supplies and Accounts, and told him that his job was to see to it that ships of the fleet got what they needed.***

---

*The USS Northampton (CA-26) was sunk in the Battle of Tassafaronga off Guadalcanal the night of 30 November-1 December 1942. Near the end of the battle, the cruiser was struck by two torpedoes which tore a large hole in her port side. She sank about three hours later as a result of progressive flooding.
**Lieutenant Commander John J. O'Donnell, USN.
***Rear Admiral William B. Young, Supply Corps, USN, served as Chief of the Bureau of Supplies and Accounts from June 1942 to March 1945. In 1941, at the time Admiral King was serving as Commander in Chief Atlantic Fleet, Young was the Atlantic Fleet supply officer with the rank of commander.

Libby #1 - 49

Q: How did you happen to get the assignment to the Northampton?

Admiral Libby: When you take an engineering postgraduate course, in those days, you were a slave of the Bureau of Engineering for a limited period thereafter. You had to do a certain amount of engineering duties in compensation for your postgraduate course.

Q: I see.

Admiral Libby: So I had another hitch of engineering duty. And there was nothing very memorable about that year, as I recall it, except we ended up out in Honolulu, one of the first ships to be overhauled in Pearl Harbor Navy Yard. We didn't stay out there very long. The most memorable thing about that was that when I got detached from the Northampton and was ordered back to Washington, I came back in the Lurline, by myself. First time I'd ever been on a sea voyage aboard a luxury liner. A wonderful five days; I thoroughly enjoyed it. Then we went back to the IC section; this was '39, wasn't it? Interior communications and fire control division—IC and FC section of the bureau—by then it was the Bureau of Ships.

Q: Yes. The interior communications section, is that ...

Admiral Libby: Interior communications and fire control, IC and FC.

Libby #1 - 50

Q: I see.

Admiral Libby: I guess. When did I have the electrical design section? I've forgotten that.

Mrs. Libby: Oh, that was '34 to '36, wasn't it?

Admiral Libby: Is that what it was? I guess so. That's right. Then in November of 1940, I got on a ship to England, and I went over there as an observer with the title of assistant naval attache, one of several assistants over there. I went over expecting to stay over there about six weeks, and I ended up staying over there until August of '41. And that, of course, was very interesting. We were not in the war, but England very much was. Then I got ordered back to ...

Q: Before you leave that, do you have any memorable events that occurred during that period of time?

Admiral Libby: Oh, I wouldn't think so. We just traveled all over the place and looked over the effects of the mines and effects of the bombs and whatnot and war damage to British ships and tried to compile what they learned about controlling battle damage and what we could learn from it. It was a very intensely interesting period, but it was all highly technical and nothing particularly memorable about it.

Q: You were almost in the learning situation, you think, observing and--for the benefit of our Navy while you were there?

Admiral Libby: That's right. That's right. And sending information back to our Navy. Several of our people over there on this same sort of duty that I was on, I mean technically the same sort of duty, were able to ride the British ships and get out on the Mediterranean Fleet, which I didn't get to do. I was not that lucky. I spent most of my time in the country. Of course, we traveled all over the British Isles.

Q: Did Mrs. Libby go with you?

Admiral Libby: Oh, no. Heavens, no.

Q: It was a dangerous time, was it not, to be in London?

Admiral Libby: All over England, yes.

Q: Where did you live?

Admiral Libby: We lived in several places. We didn't have a--we started off living in a hotel--first time we got over we lived in the Cumberland Hotel for a couple of weeks. Later I lived in two or three different flats. Several of us would get together and rent a flat.

Libby #1 - 52

And for various reasons we would move. Finally we ended up with a flat, Number 23 Grosvenor Street, right around the corner from the embassy, which is Number 1 Grosvenor Square. And then we had two or three houses out in the country, out in Virginia Water. One was called Newpipers, and I lived out there for some time. We used to get out there weekends, generally. And we had a spare set of embassy files out there at our house in Newpipers, in case our files at the embassy got bombed, which they never did fortunately, but they could have. So we lived in either of these houses or in flats in town.

Q: Did you go through any bombing?

Admiral Libby: Oh, occasionally, yes. The embassy was very fortunate. The embassy never got a direct hit, but all around Grosvenor Square it got flattened. A corner here and over there--well, never a dull moment.

Mrs. Libby: I never have found out what happened. Admiral Stark's secretary called me at quarter to seven one morning and said, "Mrs. Libby, I just want to tell you that your husband is perfectly all right."[*]

Admiral Libby: Something had happened, but I don't know what.

---

[*]Admiral Harold R. Stark, USN, was then Chief of Naval Operations.

Q: And so you stayed there a ...

Admiral Libby: Only 'til '41, when I got ordered back to Admiral King's staff.*

Q: So on September 4th you came back to have duty with Admiral King?

Admiral Libby: That was late in August. I've forgotten the exact date when I reported. One of the amusing things about that was that one of my colleagues--Admiral King, you know, had the reputation of being a pretty tough taskmaster. And one of my friends and colleagues over in London when I got my dispatch orders said, "Well, what have you done to deserve this?"

I will admit that I left with fear and trembling. I had known Admiral King only very slightly. Not being an aviator, I had never served with him. I was a little uneasy about this set of orders, but I was very fortunate to get them, I tell you. So we reported up in Newport, and I came back here briefly first and spent a couple of weeks here getting debriefed, then I went up to ...

Mrs. Libby: You mean in Washington, Dear.

Admiral Libby: I beg your pardon. I came back to Washington, yes, and spent a couple of weeks there getting unloaded and debriefed and

---

*Admiral Ernest J. King, USN, Commander in Chief Atlantic Fleet.

Libby #1 - 54

then went up and reported to Admiral King in Newport. Meanwhile, Susie stayed down to get the house rented, or something. I've forgotten. I was assistant operations officer on the staff there in the *Augusta* and then when Pearl Harbor came, I came down to Washington with Admiral King. Right after Pearl Harbor he was made Commander in Chief U.S. Fleet. It always used to be known as CINCUS, abbreviated and pronounced "sink us," and he thought maybe that was not so good, so he changed it to "CominCh," commander in chief.

Q: Good for him.

Admiral Libby: Then the Japs having accomplished "sink us" at Pearl Harbor, he didn't think the old way was such a hot idea.

Q: You started to tell me what the offices were like when you first went down there.

Admiral Libby: Oh, well, we had a very small, very decrepit, very beat-up office--one room there, borrowed furniture that was anything but elegant. And that was it for some time. But then Admiral King started to assemble his staff, and he brought some people from Newport and some people from the fleet and some people from elsewhere, and he built himself a very fine staff in very short order. Then later on when--I've forgotten exactly when it was--Admiral Stark got orders to Commander Naval Forces Europe with headquarters in London, and Admiral

King became Chief of Naval Operations as well as Commander in Chief United States Fleet. But he had two separate staffs; one as Commander in Chief U.S. Fleet and another as Chief of Naval Operations. And he distinguished between his staff and his headquarters so that there was some differentiation between the two. People in headquarters were not on the staff, and vice versa, so he managed to keep the two of them integrated but separated, if you know what I mean. He brought in a remarkably marvelous collection of people to do the jobs that they had to do--the finest officers in the Navy. He was another man like Admiral Nimitz only perhaps more so. He had an absolutely amazing knowledge of people in the Navy. He knew them. He knew them very well indeed, and he was uncanny in his ability to pick the right man for the right job. As far as I know, he never made but two mistakes. And both of those were the result of being rather too loyal to people.

Q: Who were they?

Admiral Libby: Well, I won't mention any names, but there were two people whom he didn't choose for the right jobs. But considering the number of people that he had to place in various jobs, I think that's a remarkable record.

Q: What was your relationship with him?

Admiral Libby: Well, as I say, when we came down to Washington, I was just sort of there with him, sort of doing the errands and whatnots. And then as the staff began to assemble, and as the Combined Chiefs of Staff came into existence, then I became his aide for Joint and Combined Chiefs of Staff matters. As I say, he still had his flag lieutenant, and he still had his flag secretary. The normal staff of a flag officer is the chief of staff and aide, then his flag lieutenant who is an aide and his flag secretary who is an aide, and the rest of them are just on his staff. But I just became an aide without portfolio, neither flag secretary nor flag lieutenant. I was just his assistant for Joint and Combined Chiefs of Staff matters.

What happened was that shortly after Pearl Harbor the British arrived over here in force, led by Winston Churchill and all his top military people, and their aggregation was known as the British Chiefs of Staff Committee. We didn't have anything which was completely analogous in our organization. We had the Chief of Naval Operations and the Chief of Staff of the Army. There wasn't any Air Force, you see. And the Marines were in effect a part of the Navy. The Major General Commandant was the commanding officer of the Marine Corps. We had something called <u>Joint Action Army and Navy</u>, which was a little booklet that somebody put together that nobody had paid much attention to. It really didn't amount to anything. It was not of any great value. So we had to get together an aggregation to match the British Chiefs of Staff Committee, and that consisted of Admiral King and Admiral Stark and General Marshall.* And then, as time went on, we

---

*General George C. Marshall, Chief of Staff of the U.S. Army.

Libby #1 - 57

dragged in an Army Air Corps general to stand off with the British air marshal. But that was the beginning of our Joint Chiefs of Staff, and this organization functioned all through the war as the Joint Chiefs of Staff without any legal basis whatsoever. The Joint Chiefs of Staff were never legalized until the passage of the National Security Act of 1947.

Q: But you were getting comparable opposite numbers for the British?

Admiral Libby: That's right. Well, as I said, these first meetings were held in January 1942, and we got together over in, appropriately enough, the Public Health building, which was across the street there on Constitution Avenue, and "Beetle" Smith was the first secretary and he set up a joint staff.* That was the genesis of the Joint Chiefs of Staff, called the Combined Chiefs of Staff when we met with the British. "Beetle" Smith was the first Joint Staff secretary. I've forgotten who they dragged in from Army Air Corps to start with. General McNarney was one of the early ones; then, of course, Hap Arnold came along later.** I'd have to look it up. I've forgotten the names. But the British came over in force, as I say, and we had several meetings over at the White House and then we'd get together

---
*Brigadier General Walter Bedell Smith, AUS, secretary of the Combined Chiefs of Staff and later General Dwight Eisenhower's chief of staff in Europe.
**Major General Joseph T. McNarney, AUS, Deputy Chief of Staff, U.S. Army; General Henry H. Arnold, AUS, Chief of U.S. Army Air Forces during World War II.

Libby #1 - 58

over at the Public Health building and wrestled out the first CCS papers. CCS 1, 2, 3 and 4.

Q: CCS?

Admiral Libby: Combined Chiefs of Staff. When the British and the Americans got together, they became the Combined Chiefs of Staff. And we agreed early on to bear in mind the difficulty they had trying to fight World War I by committee, you know. They never got anywhere. Nobody ever could command anything in World War I, which was one of the reasons it was such a hell of a mess. It was agreed early on that the Combined Chiefs of Staff would try to keep unto themselves the strategic direction of the war--not let it grow into a multinational committee. It wasn't easy; first the Chinese wanted in and then everybody else wanted in. But that was kept to just those two--the strategic direction in their hands--the British and the United States. And it was at these early meetings that the edict was laid down that the defeat of Germany had number one priority, after which the defeat of Japan would be undertaken. It was agreed that the lion's share of all the war production would go to the war in Europe until Germany was defeated, after which we could start working on Japan in earnest. You see, Japan was sort of held off with one hand while we polished off Mr. Hitler. That was the result of the policy of the defeat of Germany first. And, of course, at various times, we would go to meetings of the War Production Board and the meetings of this, that, and the other wartime committee in Washington; we were pretty busy people. I recall that Henry Wallace was a representative on the War Production board. He was Vice President at the time, and having observed Henry Wallace in this capacity, I was very glad when FDR decided in his last go-around that he would dump Wallace and take Harry Truman as Vice President.

Q: Otherwise we would have had Mr. Wallace as President, wouldn't we?

Admiral Libby: We would have had Mr. Wallace, and that would have been a disaster, I think, because--not that he wasn't a very pleasant gentleman--but I don't think he was--is, he's still alive as far as I know ...*

Q: I think so.

Admiral Libby: I thought he was crazy.

Q: Did you?

Admiral Libby: My frank opinion was that the man was crazy. I didn't think he was sane. Certainly, some of the things that he did at WPB meetings would not indicate that he was too mentally stable, and some of the things he did afterwards made me glad he was not President of

---

*Henry Agard Wallace died in 1965.

the United States. But that's not particularly germane to the issue. But that was extremely interesting, that cruise I had with Admiral King then from August of '41 until March of '43. I went over to the London Conference in '42 and the Casablanca Conference in '43 with Admiral King.

Q: Can you distinguish those in your mind to describe the first one in London?

Admiral Libby: Oh, yes, very well. At the conference in London the objective was to try to determine how and when to organize an assault on the continent of Europe, trying to get back into Europe. You see, France had collapsed, and England was in grave danger of being overrun. Stalin was beating us over the head to open a second front, you know, in the west. The object of exercise then was to determine when and where we could invade Europe. That was the first go-around. General Eisenhower was sent over to plan the thing. He was then a major general. He was a permanent lieutenant colonel and a major general (temporary) in the Army in '42.

Q: And was he at that conference?

Admiral Libby: Oh, yes. He was there. I flew over with Admiral King. Steve Early and Harry Hopkins were in our plane.* Steve Early

---

*Steve Early was President Roosevelt's press secretary; Harry Hopkins was a member of the War Production Board and a special assistant to Roosevelt.

and Harry Hopkins played gin rummy incessantly all the way over and all the way back. They kept books on it, and the berating and the vituperations and the screams and yells were something to hear, and at the end I think Steve Early owed Harry Hopkins 38 cents. Or vice versa.

Q: Who else attended from the United States?

Admiral Libby: General Marshall was there, and Admiral King was there, of course. I think General McNarney represented the Army Air Corps, but I could be wrong about that. Maybe it was Hap Arnold. I don't know. And then, of course, a handful of other people. There weren't too many. And Beetle Smith, I believe, was there. And Eisenhower. I just don't remember. I'd have to look it up--who were all there. One incident that happened over there which was quite interesting and perhaps prophetic--General de Gaulle came to pay his respects to Admiral King.* Admiral King and I were staying at Claridges. We had a very swank suite at Claridges, and everything was very up and above board except the food, which, of course, was nonexistent; England was still starving to death. But one morning General de Gaulle, who was over there with the French Government in exile in England, and the British were paying for his laundry and feeding him, clothing him, and taking care of the ragtag and bobtail of the French Navy and what little they had been able to scrape out of

---
*General Charles de Gaulle, head of the Free French provisional committee.

France--living entirely on the bounty of the British Empire. General de Gaulle came to pay his respects to Admiral King, and he was about as frosty as he could possibly be. Absolutely, you know, just very, very standoffish. We next encountered him at Casablanca, and when Admiral King got around to writing his book he summarized his impressions of Charles de Gaulle by saying, "General de Gaulle was his usual disagreeable self." That's all he ever said about him.

Q: What was he wearing, de Gaulle, in those days? Did he have a military uniform?

Admiral Libby: French Army uniform, square cap. At Casablanca it was agreed that for publicity purposes and just to show that everything was on the up and up, that General Giraud, who was then in command of the French Army, charged with the defense of Casablanca, for the Vichy French, and General de Gaulle were to be photographed shaking hands.*
Well, bearing in mind that General Giraud had signed General de Gaulle's death warrant when he was in charge of the Vichy French Army, it can be understood why General de Gaulle did not care much for General Giraud. So they were photographed shaking hands. They just touched hands and if the camera didn't get it then, that's all--there was no more of this "Let's have just one more shot."

But de Gaulle was throwing his weight around over there, too. As

---
*General Henri H. Giraud, Commander of French forces in North Africa.

a matter of actual fact, Winston Churchill told de Gaulle one morning at Anfa number one, which was Winston Churchill's villa, that if he, de Gaulle, didn't produce a little cooperation and climb down off his high horse that he, Churchill, would have to find someone else to be the leader of the Free French. And you know Winston Churchill's famous remark that the greatest cross he had to bear was the Cross of Lorraine? De Gaulle was a very difficult individual.

You know, I don't often disagree with Al Wedemeyer, General Wedemeyer, who is to my mind one of the great unsung heroes of World War II, unsung hero in the sense that if Truman had listened to what Al Wedemeyer wrote in his report and paid attention to it, Red China would not exist today and the Chinese Nationalists would still be on the mainland of China.* One of the contributing factors.

Well, it's a long story. It has nothing to do with me. But Al Wedemeyer feels that de Gaulle is justified in his downcheck on Churchill and Roosevelt, that he got a dirty deal from the British and the Americans; I don't agree at all. I just don't agree at all. I think he got much more than a fair shake.

Q: Why does Wedemeyer think ...

---

*Lieutenant General Albert C. Wedemeyer, AUS, served as Chiang Kai-shek's chief of staff in China during the latter part of World War II. He was also commanding general of U.S. Army Forces in the China theater. He took over in those two roles when Lieutenant General Joseph W. Stilwell was recalled from China in 1944. His memoir is Wedemeyer Reports! (New York: Henry Holt and Co., 1958).

Libby #1 - 64

Admiral Libby: Well, I don't know quite why Al feels that, but de Gaulle feels it. He hates everything British and everything Anglo-American.

Q: Doesn't he hate everything that isn't French?

Admiral Libby: Well, he hates--I don't know about that, but he certainly has no use for either England or us. And one of the things that bites him, of course, is the fact that right after the war, England was given access to our nuclear secrets *in toto*, and France wasn't. He forgets that France was just this far from going Communist. There wasn't any permanent government in France at all. Governments might last about two weeks, maximum. Sometimes they'd fall in three or four hours. And he resents our refusal. He resents a lot of things I don't think he has any business resenting, but that's beside the point. It has nothing to do with me. It was of some interest to see the good general on those two occasions.

Q: Could we go back now to the London one. You've described who attended from the United States; I presume there were opposite numbers from Britain.

Admiral Libby: Oh, of course, Churchill was there and all the British chiefs of staff, Alanbrooke and Portal and Dudley Pound and all the rest of them.* The whole kit and caboodle. British chiefs of staff, the First Lord and the First Sea Lord. One interesting thing happened. We had dinner at the Great Hall at Greenwich, which is the headquarters of the Royal Navy, and everybody came down from London for this big dinner in the Great Hall, which is a painted hall and, of course, it has the history of the Royal Navy in drawings and murals around the wall. And in the Great Hall it's tradition that no woman had ever set foot. The First Lord of the Admiralty, Mr. Alexander, sat down and played the piano.** They had an old upright piano there, and everybody gathered around and sang, and Winston Churchill happened to look in the corridor and here were a couple of WRENS, the British equivalent to our WAVES, and he invited them in to join the singing, shattering tradition that no woman had ever set foot in the hall, but they came in and that was that. After all, since the Prime Minister invited them in, nobody could say nay.

Q: Memorable for them, I'm sure.

Admiral Libby: Memorable for everybody. That was quite an evening. I've got this. I've got a box of pictures of this whole gathering somewhere. I remember the commandant at Greenwich was a big tall Navy captain; he'd lost an eye and had a black patch on and he looked like

---
*General Alan Brooke was Chief of the Imperial General Staff; Marshal of the Air Force; Charles Portal was Chief of Air Staff; Admiral Dudley Pound was First Sea Lord.
**Albert V. Alexander, First Lord of the Admiralty.

the Hathaway shirt ad, you know, and it was quite an evening.

Q: I know you remember the decisions that were reached or strategy decided upon in the London Conference.

Admiral Libby: Well, they decided that they were going to plan for the invasion of the Cherbourg Peninsula, I think. Then it turned up that this was completely infeasible and subsequently changed to the Torch Operation, the invasion of North Africa, which took place eventually.

Q: Was the decision about North Africa made at this ...

Admiral Libby: No, no. I don't think so. I think the decision was made to try to plan to invade the Cherbourg Peninsula or something. I'm completely rusty. I don't know. I'd have to look that up. I've forgotten what decisions were made at the time. But they all had code names, of course, and I believe the first thing talked about in London---but it was changed afterwards, you see. What had been talked about in London was not feasible because of shortage of material. There wasn't enough stuff out there. So I believe that the first, I don't know, I've completely forgotten. Sledgehammer and Torch, and all the rest of these operations, but I don't remember which came first, the hen or the egg. I do remember that what was planned, what was discussed and then agreed to be explored in London did not finally take place. It was changed later. And out of the subsequent developments came the North Africa operation, but that was not what was talked about.

Q: I see. It must be fascinating, though, to be part of that kind of conference, to hear men making the fate of the world practically.

Admiral Libby: It certainly was. One of the most fascinating things about it was watching the interplay between Churchill and Roosevelt and British people and our own people and, you know, the give and take. And I remember Sir Dudley Pound one afternoon at Casablanca, he was talking about the precipitate flight of the British down the Malay Peninsula. Sir Dudley Pound said, "Huh! the Goddamned British Army was so mechanized it was not mobile." Which was exactly true. They had so much rolling stock they couldn't get it off the road. The Japs just engulfed them. Much has happened to the French in Indochina. They were not mobile either. They couldn't get off the road. The Viet Cong blocked the roads and destroyed them.

I remember one set-to between Churchill and Admiral King. King was getting very much worried about the fact that he couldn't get anything to fight the Pacific War with because of this previous agreement. And finally Admiral King just came out, flat out at one of these conferences and said, "Well, who's going to fight the Japanese?" And Churchill sort of calmed him down a bit. Admiral King was not happy about that. Some of those--distribution of shortages--in the early days of the Pacific war were operating pretty much on a shoestring, you know.

Q: What are your recollections of Roosevelt at that conference?

Admiral Libby: Roosevelt was just as he appeared on the fireside chats, you know; he was very self-assured, very sure of himself. Of course, I was very much impressed by being around a great man like that. I was not as critical in my judgment of FDR then as I am in retrospect, of course. Couldn't be expected to be, but I did note one thing, and we felt it because--Winnie Churchill would butter Roosevelt up one side and down the other, you know, and just get him purring and convince him that he was the greatest man that ever lived and then he'd ask for the fillings out of Roosevelt's teeth and get them. That's one of the reasons that 99% of our production went to the British, you see.

Q: Yes. Did anybody disagree with the President or speak up and say, "Mr. Roosevelt, you're wrong"?

Admiral Libby: Not very often. I never heard anybody disagree with him. Oh, I have too, but I mean, you know, civilian control, I mean. I don't think any military people ever tried to tell him he was wrong. But it was a very interesting period.

Libby #1 - 69

Q: Did the fact that he was not mobile ever seem to affect his personality?

Admiral Libby: Not noticeably, no. I wouldn't say so.

Q: Would he come to meetings early or leave late, or would he come at the same time in his wheelchair, or how did he appear?

Admiral Libby: He would generally be there when the meeting was convened, as I recall it. I believe he would be put, and then the meeting was assembled around him. I think that's the way it happened.

Q: That would be good psychology. Now the meeting at Casablanca was—when was the one in London?

Admiral Libby: '42. June of '42, I believe.

Q: Mid '42. And then it was six months later or so that the one was held in Casablanca. Can you describe for me where that was held?

Admiral Libby: That was held at the Anfa Hotel. Winston Churchill had villa number one, and FDR had villa number two, and the rest of us lived in the hotel, which was a very swank hotel in Casablanca. It was well removed from the town itself, out in the suburbs, and it was chosen because it was a very simple matter to keep it secure and put

Libby #1 - 70

troops around it. It was sufficiently isolated from downtown so there was no danger of getting a ground attack. The Germans never did fly over and drop any bombs on it.

Q: An airstrip near?

Admiral Libby: The nearest airstrip was somewhere downtown, but not at the Anfa Hotel. On the way to Casablanca we spent the night at Marrakech; that's on the other side of the mountains from Casablanca.

Q: You were telling me about arriving at Casablanca.

Admiral Libby: I forget where the airfield was but we---wasn't much of an airstrip, as I recall it. We proceeded, of course, from the airstrip up to the hotel. And that was the first time that I saw the unique combination that you see all over North Africa---plowing by the means of two beasts. A camel is too stupid, so they hitch a mule alongside of it. They yoke a mule and a camel to a rudimentary plow--- sort of a primitive plow---and the mule will tell the camel what to do. It works all right---but the camel hates every minute of it, of course. But one of the salient features of that meeting, as you know, the oranges, the North African, the Morrocan, the North African oranges are absolutely superb. And, of course, the poor Britishers who'd had almost nothing to eat for a long time, they were much better off then than they were before we got into the war, but they brought a ship down, they tied it up at Casablanca, and loaded it right down to the Plimsoll mark with oranges to take home.*

And the test of skill of the waiter was to impale an orange on a fork, hold it in his left hand, then take a knife in his right hand and turn the orange around to get the peel off in one continuous coil. If he ever broke it, he went back to washing dishes, I guess.

Q: Now who all attended that meeting?

Admiral Libby: Oh, I couldn't begin to give you a list of them, but it was a very high level meeting. The President was there, of course, and the Prime Minister was there, and a whole flock of hangers-on. Great big conference. I've forgotten who all--all the U.S. military high command, all the British military, and several diplomats. General Eisenhower by this time was living in his villa next door to Admiral Cunningham.** By this time Ike was a four-star general. He had been in command, he'd been the overall command of the invasion and whatnot. I remember Sir John Cunningham protesting to Eisenhower at one meeting, one social meeting, that he was getting tired of having a GI put a tommy gun in his stomach every time he went out to walk in his garden. They had adjoining villas, you see. This was part of the

---

*The Plimsoll mark is a mark on a merchant ship's side to indicate how deeply she may be loaded under various sea conditions, depending on season and geographical area. In other words, the British were putting the maximum amount of cargo aboard.
**Admiral Andrew B. Cunningham, RN, commander of Royal Navy forces in the Mediterranean.

Libby #1 - 72

protection for General Eisenhower. After the Casablanca meeting, we went over to call on Eisenhower with Admiral King, and that's when this episode took place. Haven't thought much about this lately, and I'm a little rusty in my recollections of it.

Q: I had understood, if it might jog your memory, that one of the purposes was if we were going to give up making a second front this early in the war, what could the Allies do to take the pressure off Russia? And that Churchill got the agreement that we would start going into Sicily and going up what he was calling the soft underbelly of Europe.

Admiral Libby: That's right.

Q: Do you recall any of that discussion?

Admiral Libby: I would not like to be quoted at the moment. I've forgotten. I know that he, for a long time, advocated the soft underbelly approach and he was overruled for various reasons. I mean he didn't succeed in selling it to the Combined Chiefs of Staff. And as it turned out, you'll recall, that Sicily-Salerno underbelly was anything but soft. Some of the roughest fighting in the whole deal was that Sicily-Salerno business, particularly Salerno, Anzio, and that area.

Libby #1 - 73

Q: Useless and tragic and dreadful waste—loss of life.

Admiral Libby: Of course, the preliminary palaver was going on about how to get together with Joe Stalin and try to get something out of—try to get Joe to let us fly airplanes into northern Russia, all that kind of stuff, and they never got anything out of Stalin at all.

Q: Were there representatives of Russia at that?

Admiral Libby: No, they weren't there, but there was a lot of discussion about it. It was at Casablanca, I believe, that the decision was reluctantly made by Roosevelt and Churchill to knock off the Murmansk convoys. You know about those, of course. There were convoys around the northern part of Europe and into Murmansk. The ice was so far south that year that there was only 30 miles of water between the ice pack and upper Norway. Full of submarines and within easy range of the German bombers; only about 5% of the ships ever got through. They took an awful beating. And when they got to Murmansk, the Russians wouldn't unload them. They were scared to get out and face the bombings. So they were knocked off finally. They knocked it off, and they didn't even tell Stalin they were going to do it. They decided not to send any more. There was a discussion about whether we would have the operation at Burma. Lord Louis Mountbatten was to be in charge of that, but that never happened either. That expedition opened the Burma Road. A lot of things were discussed that were subsequently called off.

Q: My reading would indicate that the first time the phrase "unconditional surrender" of Japan and Germany was decided on was at this Casablanca conference.

Admiral Libby: Could have been. I don't remember. I think it was, as a matter of fact, I think Roosevelt came up with that.

Q: It always has offended me that so much of our priority for DEs and ASW went to Europe that when we needed them for a landing--needed landing craft and so on in the Pacific that we just plain didn't have any.* Didn't have enough.

Admiral Libby: Well, we had two major problems early in the war. One was this business of CCS-1--the first Combined Chiefs of Staff paper-- agreed principal enemy. Everything necessary for the defeat of Germany was number one priority, and everything else was second. That was agreed on early in January 1942 at one of the White House meetings. That was one difficulty we had and one reason why we couldn't get valves or anything else to build destroyers. Admiral King was very perturbed, because he wanted to divert sufficient of our war production to critical things like valves and piping to make escort ships so we would have some chance of getting ships to England

---
*DEs--destroyer escorts; ASW--antisubmarine warfare.

rather than having them sunk in the middle of the Atlantic. He thought it made more sense to protect the ships adequately than it did to devote all our production ability into material, then put it in ships and then have them sunk in the middle of the Atlantic Ocean. But he never succeeded in getting the Combined Materials Allocation Committee's approval. That's where we had the trouble.

Q: Who were they?

Admiral Libby: British and Americans. Mostly British over here to pick off the cream of all our production.

Q: And they were permanently here, in Washington?

Admiral Libby: Oh, heavens yes. They just came over and moved in and sat down in Washington. They watched what was coming out; they had first dibs on the production line. That was a part of the system. Once in a great while we'd be able to wangle something out of the CMAC for our Navy. But it never lasted more than about four hours, because the minute news came out the decision of the CMAC that we could have X valves or Y pieces of pipe, or so on and so forth, Winnie Churchill would pick up the phone and called FDR at the White House, and inside a half an hour the decision was reversed--give it to England.

Q: How could he?

Libby #1 - 76

Admiral Libby: Well, Winston would say, "Now, Franklin, you know what a wonderful guy you are." "Remember this piece of paper that says defeat of Germany is number one priority?"

Q: But it was a loss of so many of our boys because we didn't have the proper equipment.

Admiral Libby: That's right. But you can't have everything and somebody has to get it. It's very easy to criticize from hindsight.

Q: Oh, of course. Do you have any other recollections of the conferences, because I want to read something here that might jog your memory a little bit. But first, my information says that you received the gold star in lieu of a fourth Legion of Merit as aide to Admiral King. But it's the first reference I have to Legion of Merit and I wondered what the first three were?

Admiral Libby: Oh, I don't know. Something to do with the Pacific war probably. I got that one later, when I came back in '44.

Q: I'd like to read the citation. It says that "Displaying sound judgment and outstanding ability he [that's you] proved of invaluable assistance to the Commander in Chief, United States Fleet at the outset of the war. In his capacity as aide he provided necessary information and data which were essential to the Commander in Chief,

U.S. Fleet, as a member of the Joint Chiefs of Staff, of the Combined Chiefs of Staff and at the great meeting of the Chiefs of Government of the Allied Powers at Casablanca." And then it goes on to say, "As senior U.S. member of the Joint Staff Planning Committee for March 3rd to October 10th, 1945, he continued his outstanding service, exercising a nicety of judgment and by exhibiting unusual knowledge, loyalty, perseverance, and zeal, thereby contributing materially to the prosecution of the war."

Admiral Libby: That's when I was senior Navy member of the Joint War Plans Committee.

Q: So they're combining in the citation ...

Admiral Libby: They put them all together.

Q: ... two different jobs. I wondered if you might expand on the information that the citation contains in providing information it says.

Admiral Libby: Oh well, that's a fine way of saying that I was number one grocery clerk for the Joint and Combined Chiefs of Staff to start with. Then I was a member of the Joint War Plans Committee where we drew up war plans. The committee consisted of Bill Bessell of the

Libby #1 - 78

Army, Frank Everest of the Army Air Corps and I, and our staffs.* We were just a ...

Q: This was after you'd been out in the Pacific and ...

Admiral Libby: This is when I came back, October '44, and this lasted until the end of the war.

Q: Well, to perhaps backtrack to your next duty after you left Admiral King.

Admiral Libby: I went out and took command of Destroyer Squadron One, went up to the Aleutian Islands and was present for the Attu campaign and the Kiska fiasco. Then I got ordered to take command of new Destroyer Squadron 56, and came back and got aboard the Newcomb up in Boston in January and proceeded on out to the Pacific.

Q: Now are you getting ahead of me?

Admiral Libby: No, I don't think so.

Q: Because you're going to tell me, I hope, in detail about Attu and Kiska and who was in charge and what was accomplished, and tell me

---

*Brigadier General William W. Bessell, Jr., U.S. Army; Brigadier General Frank F. Everest, Jr., U.S. Army.

about it.

Admiral Libby: Oh well, we finally got Attu, but didn't accomplish anything at Kiska, because the Japs had evacuated, we found out before we got around to invading it.

Q: Could you start now from where did you take off and what happened and who all was there and who was in command and give me this in detail? You're the first person that I've interviewed that was related to the Alaskan operation.

Admiral Libby: Well, I don't remember too much of details about it, but Admiral Rockwell was in overall command with headquarters at Dutch Harbor.* I had Squadron One, and we had two or three of the old battleships up there. As a matter of fact, I haven't thought about this for a long time, I'll have to check up on it before I give you details. I know most of the time was spent wandering around the Bering Sea, patrolling back and forth. Attu was one of our earliest amphibious operations, and we didn't know anything about amphibious operations at all. I remember that the Army trained their troops in the desert for the Attu operation, and in order to camouflage where they were going, they gave them nothing but warm-weather clothing to wear. They didn't even have any socks, and most of the casualties on

---
*Rear Admiral Francis W. Rockwell, USN, Commander Amphibious Force North Pacific.

Libby #1 - 80

Attu were frostbitten feet. But this is so long ago I've forgotten even where we sailed from.

Libby #2 - 81

Interview Number 2 with Vice Admiral Ruthven E. Libby, U.S. Navy (Retired)

Place: Admiral Libby's home in Coronado, California

Date: 15 March 1970

Subject: Biography

Interviewer: Commander Etta-Belle Kitchen, U.S. Navy (Retired)

Q: Would you like to pick up, Admiral Libby, with your assignment in March, 1943 as Commander Destroyer Squadron One?

Admiral Libby: It was a long time ago. I'll tell what I can remember of it. I was detached from Admiral King's staff and came across from Washington to Los Angeles by train and then came down to San Diego and got aboard the Hull and went up and picked up the Phelps at Long Beach.* The Phelps was my flagship. In due course, we sailed from Long Beach with, I believe, some of the amphibious ships which were going to be escorts for the transports. We proceeded up to Cold Bay, Alaska, where none of us had ever been before. I remember that the whole expedition was supposed to be very hush-hush. It was one of our earliest amphibious operations, and these were Army troops, not Marines. In order to keep their destinations secret, the Army troops were trained for operations in Attu somewhere in the Mojave Desert, or some such place, and all they had was tropical clothing. When we

---
*Captain Libby was detached in March 1943 from the staff of Admiral Ernest J. King, USN, Commander in Chief, U.S. Fleet, and reported that same month for duty as Commander Destroyer Squadron One.

sailed from Long Beach, it was perfectly evident that everyone on the beach knew---and when we finally got up and the landing was effected at Attu, most of the casualties were from frozen feet.

Q: Did they never get cold weather gear?

Admiral Libby: Yes, they flew in wool socks and dropped them to them. The main difficulty was with frozen feet as far as the soldiers were concerned. We got up to Cold Bay about mid-April, and, of course, we were all wrapped up in anything warm we had. We didn't have any decent cold weather clothing---nothing but our blue uniforms and some sort of makee-learn windproof stuff which you couldn't wear because it was really windproof.* Your shoes would fill up with perspiration after you had this stuff on for about two hours---no ventilation in it. It was absolutely airtight.

At any rate, we were all shivering and shaking on the bridge as we put into Cold Bay, and here came this tug out to greet us with the crew of the tug in their undershirts, so apparently they were pretty much polar bears. It was warm weather for them. It was, maybe, 40; it was cold for us but warm for them. We stayed in Cold Bay for a while and went for a couple of exercises of a minor nature---sort of figuring how to get in and out of the place. In due course, the force was assembled, and we proceeded on out to the Attu occupation, the seizure of Attu.

---
*"Makee-learn" is a Navy slang term for someone or something still in the development or learning process.

I remember we started off and came out of Cold Bay in the middle of a snowstorm and pretty quickly ran into absolutely blinding fog, really pea-soup fog. All we had in those days was the old SC radar, one of the earliest radars we had. The Phelps was the only ship in my squadron that had any. They didn't have any PPIs at all, just the range scale.* You got your bearing by turning your antenna around, and then you would get a signal, and then you'd get your distance, of course, on the A scale, but there wasn't any plan position indicator. You just got an increase in amplitude in the signal when you got an echo, so it was very elementary.

Q: Did you have any people trained who knew how to use it?

Admiral Libby: Oh, yes. The radar operators were all right, but it wasn't very helpful. The Phelps was the only ship in my squadron that had any radar at all, and I was trying to get these boys positioned on the screen around the transports, and everybody was having a hell of a time. You couldn't see your nose in front of your face; it was an absolutely blinding fog.

Q: Was Admiral Kinkaid in charge of the operation?

---

*PPI stands for plan position indicator, a type of radar scope which gives a picture with a chart-like appearance, as if someone were looking down on the scene from above with his own ship in the middle. The older type A scope merely had a single horizontal scale on which targets were indicated in terms of range and relative size by deflections in the horizontal presentation. A PPI thus made it far easier to visualize the tactical situation.

Libby #2 - 84

Admiral Libby: Admiral Kinkaid was the overall commander; Admiral Rockwell had, I believe, the amphibious troops.* As I say, we started off in a dense fog, and sometime in the night the Macdonough managed to collide with the Sicard and practically cut it in two.** The Sicard managed somehow to get back to port, and the Macdonough was pretty thoroughly damaged.

Q: Hadn't the Macdonough been your ship at one time?

Admiral Libby: I had been the exec of it. The skipper of the Macdonough subsequently had another collision, and after that he was, I believe, relieved of command. He was sort of the cowboy type, charging along at high rates of speed in a blinding fog--that kind of stuff that wasn't so hot.*** At any rate, that was about the only untoward incident.

We got out and finally found our way into the transport area more by guess and by God than any other way. The transports anchored. Because we had this radar aboard the Phelps, we were sort of a mother hen. We would get the boats from the transports and lead them in to the landing area, then go back with the boats to the transports, and we spent the night running back and forth in this absolutely dense fog

---

*Rear Admiral Thomas C. Kinkaid, USN, Commander North Pacific Force; Rear Admiral Francis W. Rockwell, USN, Commander Task Force 51 (Assault Force).
**The collision occurred 10 May 1943. Both destroyers had to undergo shipyard repairs because of the extent of the damage.
***The commanding officer of the Macdonough was Lieutenant Commander Erle V. Dennett, USN.

leading the boats in to the shore. We would get as close to the beach as we dared—maybe something like 2,000 yards—and tell them, "Go that way." We kept this up all the first night and most of the next day. At one point, the fog lifted when we were on the inboard leg of this, and when we saw where we were, we were scared to death. It looked like we were practically on the beach. It was pretty rugged. The mountains are high, and the water is deep right in close to shore.

Q: At least your radar worked successfully.

Admiral Libby: Yes. Within its limitations it was all right, but it was pretty limited. The PPI didn't come out until later on in the war.

We had a lot of difficulty with the Japanese mortars when it did get clear enough so that we could sort of stand by and assist the troops on the beach with gunfire support. The Japs had the landing beach pretty well dusted up with the mortars that they had, and they would lob shells down. It was very difficult to find where the mortars were located. The Japs had this short-range but very effective mortar that they used very effectively during the war. The Marines later on developed a radar device which would locate the firing position of the mortar so they could destroy it. They would just backtrack on the trajectory with this radar. We didn't have any at this particular time, and the mortars were a damned nuisance. I don't think they killed too many people, but they harassed the beaches and they were a very unpleasant thing.

Douglas Fairbanks, Jr., was in command of one of the landing craft, as I recall it, on this particular landing.* There wasn't too much further to tell about this, except as far as we were concerned, we did a lot of gunfire support from getting into the beach as close as we could get. We would shoot up the beach with our guns and with our 40-millimeters in support of the troops. We could come within a couple of hundred yards ahead of our own soldiers without hitting them, so it was very effective. We used to go back and forth from the north side of the island, up around Chichagof Harbor, on down to Massacre Bay, and rearm frequently. The NGLOs, naval gunfire liaison officers, used to work with us by voice radio. Every time we went down to Massacre Bay to get more ammunition aboard, we would send for these boys, bring them aboard, and process them. We would send their clothes to the laundry and give them a hot shower, a good meal, and send them back with clean clothes and well fed; they enjoyed that thoroughly. That would happen about every three or four weeks or so.

Q: What was their job?

Admiral Libby: They were naval gunfire liaison officers on the beach, and they would tell us what target to shoot at and spot our gunfire

---

*Lieutenant Douglas E. Fairbanks, USNR, son of a movie actor and himself a noted actor. Fairbanks maintained his association with the Naval Reserve and eventually reached the rank of captain.

for us. They were the people from whom we got our orders to take various targets under fire.

Q: What had been their training?

Admiral Libby: They were Marines.

Q: Had you had any training or experience in amphibious operations before this?

Admiral Libby: No, this was all new. We were learning it all the hard way. It wasn't until about the early Thirties that the Navy ever did anything about amphibious operations. But all we had were motor launches. We didn't have any special landing craft, and the motor launches were completely unsuitable. They had a big landing over in Lahaina about '34, at one time.* The surf came up, and about half of the motor launches broached and were capsized and sunk. They didn't kill anybody, but it's a God's wonder that they didn't.

That is the source of a very interesting story. The Maryland, I believe, had a company of Marines aboard, and they were going to take part in a landing exercise. They also had a brigadier general in the Marine Corps. Somebody had the idea that it would be a good idea to make a cargo net, half out of manila and half out of wire. The wire

---

*Lahaina Roads, off the Hawaiian island of Maui, was a frequent U.S. Navy operating area in the 1930s.

was to run athwartships, and the manila was to run up and down. The idea was to throw the thing over the side, and the Marines would climb down like a multiple ladder and embark in the motor launches from that thing. This was the project--they were trying to make it aboard the <u>Maryland</u>, and it was a very difficult thing to make. One Saturday afternoon, this little sailor was working on this thing up at the forecastle, doing extra duty, I guess. The Marine brigadier general, the executive officer, and the first lieutenant came up, looked at this thing--none of the sailors on board had ever seen a one-star Marine before. They didn't know what this guy was; he didn't mean anything to them. They knew he was a Marine, that was all. The exec, the first lieutenant, and the brigadier general discussed this thing, and the general turned to this sailor and he said, "What do you think about this? Do you think it will work? I don't think it's going to work, do you?"

The sailor looked at him and said, "It doesn't make any difference what you think, Marine, the boatswain said make it."*

Q: That's a good story. Marvelous training, wasn't it?

Admiral Libby: Attu was eventually occupied. There wasn't too much spectacular about it, except we narrowly missed getting torpedoed once by some Japanese planes out from Paramushiro. We were doing gunfire

---

*The ship's boatswain was a warrant officer, considerably below a brigadier general in rank.

support up at Chichagof Harbor. The Army Air Corps were flying P-38s out of Dutch Harbor---these airplanes that looked like two airplanes glued together, weird-looking jobs---and they had a bandolier of .50-caliber ammunition and a couple of bombs in them.* The Army Air Corps pilots could fly, but they couldn't navigate; they didn't know anything at all about navigation. We had an old PBY, an old Catalina, an old mother hen, that used to get airborne, and lead these kids out the length of the Aleutian Island chain, Attu being the westernmost island in the lot.** The PBY would circle around, and these kids would go in and make their diving runs and their machine gun strafing runs, and they would gather up behind the old mother hen and be led back to Dutch Harbor. They always used to drop their belly tanks just before they went in to make their strafing run (wing tanks---they had enough petrol to get out there and some reserve). They would drop their belly tanks and go in and do their 20 minutes of attack, then form up behind the old mother hen and go back to Dutch Harbor. This particular afternoon we were sitting there, fat, dumb, and happy; the Phelps and three or four other destroyers; our support section was off Chichagof Harbor. The P-38s were in bombing and strafing the Japs on the beach, attacking the church which turned out to be the Japanese strong point, of course. It was full of everything the Japs had---all sorts of people and ammunition. Somebody said there was an airplane off to the west of us, and nobody paid too much

---
*P-38s were pursuit planes with twin booms leading from the fuselage back to the tail.
**The PBY Catalina was a Navy seaplane patrol bomber.

attention to it. All of a sudden, a couple of these things appeared, and they dropped what we thought were their belly tanks. The quartermaster aboard the Phelps took a look and said, "Jesus Christ, those belly tanks are under way." Torpedoes. The Jap planes had come from Paramushiro. I stood on the bridge of the Phelps and watched four torpedoes go right under the Phelps; they ran on and exploded harmlessly. Apparently, the pilots thought we were cruisers and set the torpedoes to run too deep, so they went under us.

We found out what happened later. Our forces had picked up the planes by radar down south of the island, and they put the warning out on TBS.* My division commander down there grabbed the nearest thing he had, TBS, and told us the planes were coming, but we didn't get the transmission because the mountains interfered. So they caught us completely by surprise, but they didn't do any damage to us.

Q: Did they get away safely?

Admiral Libby: We shot one of them down from the bridge of the Phelps with our number two 20-millimeter cannon on the port bow. I think we shot another one down, too. They either ran out of gas or got fouled up with bad weather; none of them ever got back to Paramushiro. We found that out later, after the war. They came out and made a manful attack, but it didn't do them any good.

---

*TBS--talk between ships, which was voice radio.

Q: It was well conceived, I must say.

Admiral Libby: Oh, yes, but none of them made it. The only casualty aboard the Phelps was that this airplane came boiling up the port side and strafed us with its machine guns, rat-tat-tat, and made several holes in the port side of the hull. One of the bullets came through and buried itself in the platen of the typewriter of the yeoman who was sitting in the office, and the yeoman fainted. But nobody got a scratch.

Q: You were lucky that day.

Admiral Libby: We certainly were. We must have led a pure life to produce that. We had a total of three movies aboard the Phelps, and we used to show movies in the afternoon, because we didn't want to show them after dark---darken ship. We couldn't have them abovedecks. So we would have all the wardroom would hold every day, from about 2:00 to 3:30---people off duty and whatnot. One of the three movies we had was this Mary Martin movie, "Kiss the Boys Goodbye."* We showed that thing every third day for about four months, and everybody went, and nobody ever got tired of looking at it. They could tell everything that was going to happen.

---

*"Kiss the Boys Goodbye" was a 1941 film also starring Don Ameche and Oscar Levant.

Q: Expand further, why they liked it and about how she was dressed.

Admiral Libby: I remember one scene, Mary Martin is dressed up in some sort of a southern belle crinoline job, a very elaborate gown, up on the springboard getting ready to dive into a pool, I believe it was. And just before she dove into the pool, she suddenly dropped this dress, and she had a bathing suit underneath it.

Q: I think you told me the boys hoped every day that she would forget the bathing suit.

Admiral Libby: I think they hoped every day that she would forget her bathing suit--very popular.

Q: That was when she sang, "My Heart Belongs to Daddy."

Admiral Libby: That's right. We hung around up there for some time trying to get enough stuff together to proceed with the invasion of Kiska. We spent a long time patrolling back and forth in the Bering Sea, patrolling against submarines. We never did see any submarines. The weather varied from terrible to worse most of the time until in the early spring. During the early part of our stay up there, the Dale had an appendicitis case aboard. The Dale had permission to leave the screen and get on an easier course so the surgeon could operate on this kid. They took off on the easiest course they could find; none of it was good—a very rough life. They rejoined the next morning, and I sent a message over asking how the patient was. The message came back that the patient was fine, so I sent back, "How is the doctor?"

The answer came back something like, "The doctor is tired but triumphant." I wouldn't have cared to have operated on anybody for a hangnail; it was really rough and nasty that night.

It was boring patrolling back and forth, refueling from the tanker, and this kind of stuff.

Q: It was a terribly important part of history.

Admiral Libby: Fueling at sea was relatively new, and we had a technique which somebody had worked out which required that you take a towline and be towed by the ship from which you are fueling. I remember one time we got the Phelps alongside the Pennsylvania, one of the old battlewagons we had up there, and it was just absolutely impossible to keep on this towline. We couldn't get it rigged the right length and practically ripped the bow out and banged into the Pennsylvania a half a dozen times. (We didn't do it, but almost).

Q: You're under way all the time, in very bad, heavy seas?

Admiral Libby: Oh, yes. The standard up there. We finally gave up trying to do it on the towline. Somebody said, "Let's try it without the towline." So we tried it without a towline and had no trouble at all. It wasn't very long thereafter that the practice of taking the towline was abandoned completely. We'd just steam up alongside and hold the ship in position, and get the burtoning gear over and the hoses over, but the towline was abandoned.* It was completely unnecessary and dangerous in bad weather.

Q: It's interesting that you were the first ones to do it.

Admiral Libby: I'm not sure we were the first, but I know that we managed to fuel this particular day without using the towline, because it was impossible to use a towline. You simply couldn't control the ship at all; it was like a bucking bronco.

When we finally did get around to the invasion of Kiska, we found that the Japs had all evacuated and gone. But in the harbor in Kiska the Abner Read hit a mine and blew its stern off and we lost about 24 or 30 people in the middle of the night, pitch blackness, but that was the only casualty.** When the people got ashore in the first dawn, they found the Japs long gone. I don't know when they got away, the date of evacuation. I think shortly after the Komandorski Island battle, probably.***

---

*Burtoning gear was a wire rope with pulleys on it. The fueling hose was suspended from this rig which connected the two ships.
**On 18 August 1943, an underwater explosion blew off the stern of the destroyer Abner Read (DD-526) resulting in one known dead, 34 wounded, and 70 men missing and presumed dead.
***The Battle of the Komandorski Islands was fought on 27 March 1943.

They had something up there which they called the "battle of the pips," I remember.

Q: What does that mean?

Admiral Libby: Radar was rudimentary, and you got some very strange echoes sometimes. Some of the battleships shot up an awful lot of ammunition one night at what they thought was a Japanese sweep, and it turned out to be false radar echoes. They called it the battle of the pips.* It may have been during that that the Japanese evacuated Kiska. I have forgotten all of the details on these things. At any rate, when we got our troops there, the Japanese were long gone.

Q: How long were you in the Aleutian campaign?

Admiral Libby: We were up there from early April through September of 1943.

Q: This occasion was the awarding of your first Legion of Merit, of which you got six. It says, "For exceptionally meritorious conduct as destroyer squadron commander during the seizure and occupation of enemy held Attu Island in May, '43, and later of Kiska Island. In command of a fighter support unit covering transports and initial

---

*See Bruce McCandless, "Battle of the Pips," U.S. Naval Institute Proceedings, February 1958, page 660.

landings in the Holtz Bay area and later in complete control of patrolling vessel operations, he furnished an outstanding example of efficiency. Attacked on one occasion by enemy submarines, he skillfully directed his destroyer squadron in the inflicting of damage of one undersea craft and the probable sinking of another, escaping with no damage to our forces."

Admiral Libby: I had forgotten about that. I know the Monaghan chased one submarine up on the beach one night south of Kiska, and I know that every time we came in and out of Sand Bay the Army Air Corps would sight a submarine and we'd go look for it and never found one there. There was something on the bottom that looked like a submarine to the Army Air Corps, and every time we'd go in and out of Great Sand Bay, we'd get a submarine alarm from them.

There weren't too many Jap submarines up in the Aleutian Islands around this time. I don't think they liked it up there very well.

Q: I wouldn't imagine it would be very good operations up in that area for anybody, let alone a submarine.

Admiral Libby: It was probably better for submarines than for surface craft. I don't know how sonar conditions up there were. We had a lot of trouble--there were a lot of wrecks around there. They weren't too well charted. Off Holtz Bay we had to go in periodically for gunfire support, and it's a little difficult to determine exactly where you are. It's low visibility, and you can't see too well. There was this one particular wreck, and I'll bet you that in the _Phelps_ we made ten attacks on this thing over a period of two or three weeks. We'd get a beautiful echo, then you'd get a nice doppler on it from the strong currents, and you'd think you were at anchor and you'd be sliding by the thing at about eight knots.* We let go more depth charges on this bleeding wreck--it fooled us repeatedly. It gave a very fine echo, but we never did any real damage to the wreck, I don't think. It cost us quite a few depth charges.

My recollection of detail up there is a little fuzzy after all these years. It was a very monotonous time charging back and forth. I do remember one time after we had been out patrolling Bering Sea for several weeks, we went back to Dutch Harbor for some reason, and I was invited up on the hill to Admiral Kinkaid's to have lunch. Captain Entwistle was chief of staff to Admiral Kinkaid.** Before lunch he gave me a can of beer. I drank the beer, and I had bells ringing and buzzing in my head. I was as looped as I could possibly be, on one can of beer. I hadn't had any alcohol for weeks.

Here's the funny thing about that campaign up there. All through the spring and until mid-summer you can have some beautiful weather up there--we did at mid-summer--we also had bad weather. We were all soaking wet all the time and cold and miserable, and nobody in the

---

*Doppler was the change in pitch of the sonar ping returned from the target, indicating relative motion between ship and target.
**Captain Frederick I. Entwistle, USN, chief of staff to Commander North Pacific Force.

squadron had a cold. Nobody. We hadn't been down in Honolulu more than about 20 minutes when about half the squadron came down with bad colds.

Q: How did the doctor explain that?

Admiral Libby: It was too cold for any cold germs to flourish up in the Aleutians, and we got down in the semi-tropics and everybody was laid low by them.

Q: It's possible because of the less dense population that there really were fewer germs in the air.

Admiral Libby: There probably were fewer, but I think they were perhaps inert. They didn't incubate in the cold air.

When we left, we escorted eight or 12 merchant ships down from Dutch Harbor to Pearl. We had a little difficulty with them getting them not to show lights at night.

Q: What were they carrying?

Admiral Libby: Nothing. They had discharged their cargo and were going back to Pearl Harbor, bare boat. I didn't think it was such a hot idea to have them show lights at night and I couldn't get them to darken ship without a lot of trouble, but I finally made it. We got down there without coming to blows or having to sink any of them for misbehavior, but they were a pretty maverick lot.

We were very, very irked about one thing up there. As I say, being constantly on patrol and being constantly under way, we had to refuel quite frequently, and we did it under way from some of the bigger ships, if they were available, or there was a tanker which was anchored in Great Sand Bay. We used to duck in there to fuel on occasion. This was a commercial tanker, chartered by the Navy but not Navy manned--civilian manned and a civilian tanker. These people were getting extra money for being in a war zone--something like $100 a day extra money for being present in a war zone. All kinds of incentives to get them to brave the dangers of the Aleutian Islands in wartime. If we got in after 4:00 o'clock in the afternoon or before 8:00 o'clock in the morning to fuel from this particular beast, we had to put our own people aboard to man the hoses and turn the valves. The crew wouldn't work after 4:00 o'clock.

Q: Working an eight-hour day?

Admiral Libby: An eight-hour day.

Q: Could you have forced them to fuel you?

Admiral Libby: I don't think so. It was simpler to put our own people aboard. They would let our people go aboard and turn the valves. That burned us up. I've forgotten what ship that was, but we took a rather dim view of that.

Q: Were you still on the Phelps when you went down to Pearl?

Admiral Libby: Yes.

Q: Can you tell me something about your experiences when you were around Pearl? You arrived in Pearl from Alaska in September 1943.

Admiral Libby: We were detailed to escort a carrier task force down for a raid at Wake Island. We had six carriers in a circular cruising formation. I had the screen; I was on about circle eight somewhere, which means about 8,000 yards, four nautical miles, from the formation center. Admiral Montgomery was in command of the task force.* We proceeded on down, and the carrier planes went in and raided Wake Island; they came back, and we went back to Pearl. And that's about all there was to that as far as I was concerned, except the usual business of escorting and refueling, and getting the ships around, and that sort of thing.

Q: Had you ever seen a task force the size of this one at Wake Island before?

---

*Rear Admiral Alfred E. Montgomery, USN, Commander Task Force 14. The raid on Wake was made 5-6 October 1943 by planes from the carriers Essex (CV-9), Yorktown (CV-10), Lexington (CV-16), Independence (CVL-22), Belleau Wood (CVL-24), and Cowpens (CVL-25).

Admiral Libby: Yes, I think so. This wasn't a particularly big task force. As I recall, we had about six carriers, two or three cruisers, and something like 18 destroyers. The circular fleet formation was just coming into its own, really. It was worked out and turned out to be a very easily maneuvered, very flexible, very fine method of cruising with a task force at sea. You change courses simply by simultaneous ships' turns---every ship just turns and the whole thing moves around. You had good antisubmarine protection, and you've got room inside it so that the carriers can turn into the wind to launch and recover aircraft without everybody else having to move all over the place. The carriers just run around inside the movable circle, more or less independently with their own plane guards if they had them. We didn't have helicopters in any large numbers, if we had them at all.

Q: This is really the beginning of the system which became such a successful maneuver, all across the Pacific.

Admiral Libby: That's right, this was the early days of the circular cruising formation. I don't know that it was the first, because I was a Johnny-come-lately in getting to sea. I didn't get to sea until March of '43, when the war had been going on for some time. It certainly was the cruising formation that we used almost exclusively in all the operations that I took part in from then on. It had been pretty well proved out and pretty well standardized.

One of the things that I remember most about this trip to Wake was that our station was at least 8,000 yards from Admiral Montgomery's flagship, and he loved to put out his night orders by flaghoist.* We were so located that along about evening, when he started putting out his night orders, he would run up the flags, and we would lose them completely in the setting sun--just a great glare of colors between us and the setting sun. We couldn't see anything. Then we would get on the signal light and try to get him that way, and we couldn't get him to acknowledge the signal light. In desperation I would get on the TBS and tell Admiral Montgomery that we couldn't read his signals, and would he do something about it. This went on every day. He never would do anything about it, and finally when things got really bad one night--I had a chief signalman named Jones who had been with me a long time and he was a crackerjack, one of the best signalmen in the fleet. He was up there working his tail off trying to figure out what we were supposed to do that night. We couldn't see the flaghoists, and we couldn't get Admiral Montgomery to send his orders any other way. Finally, when I protested vehemently, he called over and said, "Put competent signalman on watch." I thought Jones was going to jump overboard.

Q: He had no concept of what you were faced with, it appears.

Admiral Libby: I don't know whether he did or not. I don't think he

---

*Rear Admiral Montgomery's flagship was the USS *Essex* (CV-9).

had ever been in destroyers. I remember that difficulty very well.

Q: How did you solve it?

Admiral Libby: We just sort of got around it with the help of the other destroyers. Some of the people on the other side--we'd get the word eventually from chitchatting among ourselves. Since I was the screen commander, I felt I'd like to know what we were going to do for the night--whether we were going to change course or what. I always found out in time, but it was a laborious process sometimes.

On the Wake Island raid, we never even saw the island. They launched the planes 50 miles away. We just had a pleasant little trip down to Wake Island and back. That's about all there was to it as far as the destroyers were concerned.

After that, we went out to the Gilberts, and that was a horse of another color. That was really a workout. I again had the transport screen, and we had a good big task force with Admiral Turner in command. He proceeded to put the transports through their paces on the way down, trying to train them.* The transports, as I remember the situation, were a miscellaneous collection of ships. They were not uniform in characteristics. They were cranky to steer and cranky to handle. Their skippers were not used to staying in formation, and it took a bit of doing to break them in to cruise at sea without getting all fouled up. So the early days of the trip from Pearl on

---
*Rear Admiral Richmond Kelly Turner, USN, Commander Task Force 52 (Northern Attack Force).

Libby #2 - 104

down to the vicinity of Makin and Tarawa were spent in putting the transports through their paces and teaching them how to stay in formation and all that. I will say that Admiral Turner succeeded in getting them all down there without having any collisions.

A couple of nights before the landing, we had a mild alarm. We picked up some ships on the radar and didn't quite know what they were. We had just gotten orders from Admiral Turner to get my squadron together and go launch a torpedo attack at them. I had just broken loose from the screen and gotten formed up and started when a voice came over the TBS identifying the ships as a carrier and three or four destroyers of our own coming to join up. It was just one of those things.

On the morning of the assault, two of my destroyers were well inshore to mark the line of departure for the landing boats. (They come up to the line of departure, get all set, and then go on in.) When the landing craft had gone in, we went around to the northern end of the island to do some shore bombardment on some previously assigned targets at Makin. Bobby Griffin had the battleships, and they were down south, and we were up in this little pocket up north.* The battleships were blazing away with their 14-inch guns. But the whole island, being about as high as a table, we were getting literally dusted up by our own battleships. These 14-inch shells were falling all around us, and we didn't like it too well. We finally got the battleships to lower their sights a little bit so their shells hit the

---

*Rear Admiral Robert M. Griffin, USN, Commander Task Group 52.2 (Fire Support Group).

land instead of dropped around us. Bobby Griffin got very mad at me for protesting that he was shooting at me.

Q: How did you get to him, by voice?

Admiral Libby: Yes, TBS radio. TBS was a big help when it worked. It wasn't very reliable; it wouldn't go through a rain squall; it was an in-and-outer—sometimes it worked and sometimes it wouldn't work at all. It was shortwave, of course, and relatively low powered and yet at one time during these operations we heard a TBS conversation that turned out to be ships in West Loch at Pearl Harbor. We got some sort of peculiar bounced transmission all the way across the Pacific. But if you had a good heavy rainsquall between you and somebody talking, you'd lose him completely.

I don't remember anything very outstanding about the Makin operation except the Liscome Bay being torpedoed. About the second day of the operation, when we were standing by to do gunfire support for the troops on the beach, just at daylight there was a tremendous flash off to the west and we found out that the Liscome Bay, one of our escort carriers, had gotten a torpedo; that ship literally disintegrated. Some of DesRon 24 had been escorting her, and they never did detect any sign of a Jap submarine, but one torpedo hit the Liscome Bay. She was just a sandwich of gasoline and bombs anyway. There wasn't a piece of anything left of that ship any bigger than a tabletop. She just disintegrated. We lost Mullinnix, one of our finest young admirals, in her, and the skipper or exec was taking a shower when she went up and he was blown out into the water without a stitch of clothes on.* But he was saved; he didn't die. They lost a good two-thirds—practically all the crew.

During the pre-landing bombardment, the Japs holed up the way they always did. We made the landing, our people went on inland, everything was hunky-dory, and then they discovered that all the Japs came out of their caves after the bombardment was over and all the airplanes had gone away. When we were in this harbor on the north end there, our tanks were moving along through the jungle, and one of our tanks had about three Japs on the top and another tank came up and shot them off. That particular engagement was fairly early in our amphibious business. We learned, increasingly, as time went on, that it was absolutely impossible to put on too much preliminary bombardment, either by guns or by airplane, before a landing. Because no matter how thoroughly you thought you had blasted the place, the Japs were well dug in, and they would come out in force after you thought nothing could be alive, that nothing could have withstood the bombardment that these places went through—but they were still there, hale and hearty.

I would like to say at this point that this particular operation was the first one that I had under Admiral Turner. We went from there

---

*Rear Admiral Henry M. Mullinnix, USN, Commander Task Group 52.3 (Air Support Group). The commanding officer of Mullinnix's flagship Liscome Bay, Captain Irving D. Wiltsie, USN, was also killed when the ship was lost.

out to the Marianas campaign. I had gone back and gotten a squadron of new destroyers and reassembled them and brought them out to Pearl and then went off on the Marianas campaign, again with Admiral Turner.* Admiral Turner's first amphibious operation was Guadalcanal. He learned his trade the hard way. You know about the First Savo and what a horrible thing it was down there.** Admiral Turner was involved in a whole series of increasingly important amphibious operations, and he got increasingly proficient as time went on. I will say this about Admiral Turner--there was never any doubt in anybody's mind as to what he wanted you to do. He was a perfectly wonderful person to work for--to be with in an operation like this--because you knew all the time what he wanted done, which was a tremendous help. There is nothing worse than being supposed to do something and not knowing what you're supposed to do. That never was the case with Admiral Turner; you knew exactly what he wanted.

Q: Were you with him at Tarawa as well as Makin?

Admiral Libby: This was all one operation. We were up north; we were not down at Tarawa. The task force separated.

---
*On 16 January 1944, Captain Libby assumed command of Destroyer Squadron 56; his flagship was the USS Newcomb (DD-586).
**First Savo was a night battle off Guadalcanal the night of 8-9 August 1942. Allied Forces were caught by surprise and lost the cruisers Astoria (CA-34), Vincennes (CA-44), Quincy (CA-39), and HMAS Canberra.

Libby #2 - 108

Q: He was criticized so severely for Tarawa and the terrible loss of life there.

Admiral Libby: Tarawa had never been reconnoitered properly. All we had was some submarine photography, as I remember, and the UDT boys I don't think had had at it beforehand.* It was fairly easy, and we didn't have the underwater demolition outfits that we had later on. We just didn't know our business too well.

Q: They didn't have the topographical or oceanography information.

Admiral Libby: We didn't know much of anything about the western Pacific. It was all mandated territory; the Japs kept us the hell out of it pretty much, and we didn't know our way around.** We didn't know anything about the extent of the beach defenses, very little. The beach defenses were much more formidable than anyone imagined, and it was a bloody battle.

Q: A terrible learning process we went through.

Admiral Libby: There again, as I say, not anywhere near enough bombardment. That was really rough--that Tarawa deal. I was not there. We were up north. We were up north, because Makin was a lot

---

*UDT--underwater demolition teams.
**In the peace process following World War I, a number of Pacific islands had been mandated to the Japanese.

closer to the nearest Jap airfield than Tarawa--something like 150 miles closer, and they wanted to be sure to get that in a hurry before the Japs could react by air. At that, it took a couple of days longer than they thought it would.

Q: The experience of knowing the person you are dealing with is invaluable in something of this sort. Then did you go back to Boston to pick up the Newcomb?

Admiral Libby: Yes, I went back to Boston and went aboard her. She had just been built, and we gathered the squadron as we went along. We went down and picked up a couple in Norfolk. Then we escorted the Wasp down to Trinidad where she was going for her shakedown training. There, again, there's nothing like being stubborn, or a coward, or something. This won't make history books either, but I'll tell you what happened.

I was riding the Newcomb; Larry Cook was my flag captain.* (He lives over here in town now.) We had another destroyer with us, another one of mine, maybe two, and we were approaching the Dragon's Mouth down there at Trinidad and heading due south. According to my book we were heading right straight into the minefield; the Dragon's Mouth, according to my navigation, was 60 miles to the east, so I sent word over to the skipper of the Wasp what my navigation showed me to be, latitude and longitude, and nothing happened. We kept on heading

---
*Commander Lawrence B. Cook, USN.

south and finally in desperation I just ran up the flaghoist, "You are standing in danger"--went hard left and headed east. The Wasp apparently decided discretion was the better part of valor, because they followed me. We headed on east and later turned in and got safely into the harbor.

That afternoon I got a message from the skipper of the Wasp.* He said, "Thank you very much. My navigator was using the wrong page in the Air Almanac."

Q: It sounds like it could be something that could easily happen.

Admiral Libby: Sure. It did. Brand-new crews, you know. In Squadron 56--this was so typical, other ships were the same way in varying degrees. I was very fortunate. In my eight ships I had eight Naval Academy graduates for captains--one for each ship. In none of the ships did I have more than one other Naval Academy officer aboard. None of the execs were Naval Academy; the ships were manned 99% with reservists. They had to be--the Navy grew so rapidly. These kids with the best will in the world and absolutely miraculous morale just didn't know their jobs too well, so it was not too surprising that the navigator used the wrong page in the Air Almanac.

Q: How did you go about training these reservists? It must have been

---

*The commanding officer of the Wasp (CV-18) was Captain Clifton A.F. Sprague, USN.

a terrible responsibility to know you were operating your squadron right.

Admiral Libby: They were people who had been going to their reserve training, two weeks training a year, and drill one night a week. They were rusty.

Q: They could have come in from 90-day wonders.[*]

Admiral Libby: Sure. We had a lot of those, too. When I got out to Pearl with the Newcomb and the other three ships, we still had four to go. I was given temporary duty on the staff of Commander Destroyers Pacific Fleet, Rear Admiral Reggie Kauffman.[**] It was my job to develop a doctrine for shore bombardment by destroyers, for close gunfire support, having had considerable experience up in the Aleutian Islands with it and having made some suggestions as to how to do it. I drew up a scheme for laying out a range over on Kahoolawe Island, a little rock in the Pacific, one of the Hawaiian Islands. It's in the gap between the big island, Hawaii, and the next island to the north, Lanai. The trade winds come through that venturi, and about half the time there's a great pillar of dust blowing due west from Kahoolawe. Nobody lives on it; it's completely barren. The genesis of this field that I had to develop had hitherto just been a rather hit-or-miss job.

---

[*] Reserve officers commissioned following a 90-day training period.
[**] Rear Admiral James L. "Reggie" Kauffman, USN, Commander Cruisers and Destroyers Pacific Fleet.

Libby #2 - 112

We'd just go shoot at something without any sure idea of how accurate we were, so I got them to lay out a firing range over there with triangulated targets so we knew exactly what their latitude and longitude were. We put an observation post there so people could spot the fall of shot from the destroyers. Then I took the ships over one by one and two by two and put them through a course of sprouts over there, and it turned out to be pretty good training, very valuable training for the kids. They really learned something about close gunfire support.

Q: And there had been no real plan for this until you did it?

Admiral Libby: That's right. This was the first time we really formalized it, and later on it developed into something far more elaborate than I had time to put together, but we initiated it and got it growing.

Q: Didn't you feel a sense of satisfaction doing this?

Admiral Libby: Oh, sure. It worked out very well and it was a help. Every ship that went through Pearl, even the big ships, took the courses after that.

I remember I was a little taken aback. I had worked this thing all out, got it all laid out, written the plans for it, and then the ink was no sooner dry on the thing and the admiral had signed it when he said, "Okay, you wrote it. Now take some ships out and go try it."

Q: Didn't you expect that?

Admiral Libby: It worked fine.

Q: Did you see Admiral Nimitz during this time when you were in Pearl?*

Admiral Libby: Oh, yes. We saw him periodically. We didn't see too much of him, but we'd sit down in conferences every now and again.

Q: Do you have any comments about him?

Admiral Libby: Nothing in particular except he was his usual genial self.

Q: I've observed about him that he was always anxious to take any new idea or intelligent suggestion and put it to use. I wondered if he made any comment about this particular operation of yours?

Admiral Libby: If he did, I don't remember it. This was small potatoes actually, compared with what he had on his mind.

---

*Admiral Chester W. Nimitz, USN, Commander in Chief Pacific Fleet.

Libby #2 - 114

Q: True, but it wasn't really in the effect that it had.

Admiral Libby: It was a useful thing to do, I'm sure of that. It paid dividends, because from then on you could send any ship to do close gunfire support—he'd been through the school and knew what to do. Offhand to a layman, that sounds like a very simple thing for a ship to steam offshore or lie to offshore and shoot at the beach. But it's not that simple, because you're shooting at a fixed target but you're doing it from a moving platform, and you've got to compensate for your own motion and the current, and the wind, and the drift, and this, that, and the other. When you stop and think that as a matter of routine, we used to put 5-inch gunfire within 50 yards of our own front lines—you've got to be pretty accurate to do that.

Q: Well, to identify the target in the first place.

Admiral Libby: You had either assigned targets—the way it would work, you would have targets simply assigned by grid number. You had geographical positions which could be half a mile or a quarter mile ahead of our front lines, or someplace identified where a gun was shooting and they wanted the gun knocked out, or something like that. You would do that on assigned target, either pre-planned or just assigned. When it came to close support of your own troops, you had a spotter in the front lines, and he would spot your gunfire for you. He would start out, maybe 100 yards ahead, and move it on back, walk it back to wherever they wanted it.

Q: How did he communicate with you?

Admiral Libby: By voice radio. One very effective tactic that we used all through the Marianas campaign—we kept star shells going all night long over the Jap area, and it did two things.* It kept them awake, and made a hell of a racket. These shells came whooping down, and they scream after the parachute pops out of the star shell. I don't know how many thousands of star shells we fired during the Marianas campaign, but there were a lot of them.

Q: A terrific psychological effect, I should think.

Admiral Libby: The Japs hated it. The enemy hates this gunfire, too. The North Koreans hated it, and I'm sure the North Vietnamese hate it. They have no possible way of getting back at it. They don't know where it's coming from—they can't see the ships. The New Jersey could shoot 16 miles, 20 miles inland.**

Q: From four or five miles offshore.

---

*A star shell is a projectile that detonates in the air and releases an illuminating parachute flare.
**The battleship New Jersey (BB-62) was reactivated from the reserve fleet in order to provide shore bombardment of Vietnam.

Libby #2 - 116

Admiral Libby: Sure. There's no getting back at it. It just comes at you; you can't spot it; you can't defend yourself from it; there's nothing you can do about it; you're completely helpless.

Q: Do you hear it coming--the whistle?

Admiral Libby: Oh, yes.

Q: How far off will a destroyer shell hit?

Admiral Libby: We weren't too far offshore. We were probably a couple of thousand yards, maybe a mile, offshore.

Q: But they couldn't see you?

Admiral Libby: They could see us, but they couldn't do anything about it. Of course, down in the Palaus, to support the underwater demolition team, we practically scraped the beach. You could almost reach out and touch the beach; we weren't more than 50 yards offshore.

Q: I think this doctrine of shore bombardment is extremely interesting. How many people would even know how it was developed is questionable. You are the person that developed it.

Admiral Libby: I will probably forget when the time comes, so I'll tell you now about this very amusing experience when we went down to the Palau campaign, after the Marianas were over. We transferred from Admiral Turner's outfit to the South Pacific Force. Admiral Fort was in command of the Palau operation and we had Oldendorf, who had the battleships, Bob Hayler, and Ainsworth had the cruiser divisions--a completely new outfit as far as we were concerned.* We'd never worked with any of them before, so we had a certain amount of getting acquainted that had to be done, which we did. There was no difficulty. The Bennion, which Jock Cooper had, and the Newcomb, which I rode, were given the job of supporting the underwater demolition team two days before the landing.** We went in, as I say, and just scraped the beach, and these UDT boys went in with their wet suits, swim suits, and walkie-talkies on their back, and laid their underwater demolition charges and their Bangalore torpedoes.

Q: This was at night?

Admiral Libby: No, this was in late afternoon. They were getting some machine gun fire from somewhere in the jungle just off to the left. We took it under fire as best we could with our 40-millimeters, after we ceased firing, it opened up again. Finally one of these UDT boys with his walkie-talkie--we could hear him and talk to him from

---

*The operation took place in November 1944. Rear Admiral George H. Fort, USN, commanded Task Force 32; Rear Admiral Jesse B. Oldendorf commanded Task Force 32.2; Rear Admiral Robert W. Hayler, USN; Rear Admiral Walden L. Ainsworth, USN, was embarked in a cruiser.
**Commander Joshua W. Cooper, USN, whose oral history is in the Naval Institute collection.

Libby #2 - 118

our own voice radio aboard--said in a very irate voice to me, "You dumb son of a bitch, can't you see that the gunfire's coming from so and so?" So we attempted to cover "so and so" and when we got them all safely back in their rubber boats and back to their transport, Jock Cooper called me up on the TBS and said, "A new spotting system has been born."

Q: At that point he wasn't caring about the naval courtesy.

Admiral Libby: No, he just wanted me to get that machine gun off his back, and I don't blame him.

Q: He probably was a lot closer to it.

Admiral Libby: They were shooting at him, not us.

Q: I want to go back now to the Marianas, Saipan, and Tinian. I don't want you to leave out anything there that you can recall.

Admiral Libby: The Marianas was quite a long operation. Tinian was a pushover once we got at Tinian, but we had to take Saipan first. It's a big island, and there were thousands of Japs on it, they were all well dug in, and it was a slow and laborious operation. The transports would retire every night, they would come in during the day and keep ferrying supplies ashore and then retire every night at sunset and stand off to westward to avoid being sitting ducks or targets for submarines or Jap air if there were any around. That was always a lot of good clean fun getting the ships all formed up. Then they would come back every morning and repeat the process of unloading and reinforcing, getting the supplies ashore.

We only got bombed once, as I recall it. Just about dusk, just as we were sortieing, getting ready to depart for the night, a couple of Japs came up from Guam and dropped a few. They didn't hit anything. I don't know how they could have missed, but they didn't hit anything, and they went away.

One of my boys one night distinguished himself. We had just gotten formed up and just gotten well on our way out to sea with the transports in our particular group, and Kelly Turner called me up on voice radio and said, "There's a hole in your screen." He had a better radar than I had apparently and had spotted that there was a hole in the screen. We were just getting formed up and pitch dark; you couldn't see anything. I called the guy who was supposed to be in the screen and I said, "Your station is thus and so."

He came back indignantly, "I am in station thus and so." Still the hole persisted. So after half an hour of argument that he was not in thus and so, he rather shamefacedly called over and said, "Okay, I'm in the wrong formation." He'd gotten in the wrong group. But then he came home.

During the Marianas "Turkey Shoot," the whole kit and kaboodle of transports and screen went on around east of Saipan and stayed over there for three or four days waiting for the Marianas "Turkey Shoot" to take place.* When Spruance and his boys had shot down all the Jap airplanes we all came back and resumed the capture of the Marianas.**

Q: Were you able to see any of that?

Admiral Libby: No, they were well off to the westward. We were east. My glamorous job was simply to be a screen for the transports both at anchor and under way--I had command of the screen for the whole shindig there. I was not with Spruance's fleet at all.

Q: Your job was at Saipan.

Admiral Libby: Yes. And his job was on out. They were two completely different task forces. While we were retired and cruising back and forth, we had this motley assembly; we had a whole flock of ships--great big batch of transports and destroyers, carriers, and this, that, and the other. We were all grinding back and forth. We'd stand east, and then we'd turn around and stand west, each group on differently assigned courses just to keep out of each other's hair. It was impossible. Captain Loomis had one outfit; he was well senior to me.*** He had a group of transports, and I still had my

---

*The Marianas "Turkey Shoot" involved the shooting down of more than 300 Japanese planes by carrier pilots on 19 June 1944.
**Admiral Raymond A. Spruance, USN, Commander Fifth Fleet.
***Captain Donald W. Loomis, USN, Commander Task Group 52.4 (Transport Group "Baker").

destroyers. We were plowing along, just making holes in the ocean (this had been going on for four or five days), and finally I got a little uneasy about it because it was perfectly obvious to take a look and predict where we would be two hours from now if you'd been watching us. So I sent over to Loomis and said, "Don't you think this task force is getting in a rut?" The message had no sooner left the ship when we got a submarine contact--wham, just like that. At the same time, a couple of carriers got submarine contacts. The place was full of Jap subs that had been watching us for four or five days. We sunk one, and one of the carrier destroyer escorts sunk one. We knocked off three Jap subs that afternoon, and after that we stopped prowling the same ocean.

Q: Can you tell me about that? What was it like? Did you see any evidence of the submarine?

Admiral Libby: We knew we sunk this one, because we got bits and pieces that finally came to the surface. After we depth charged it along with one of the four-pipe destroyers (the pair of us sank it) there were two very heavy explosions.* The Japs had some device whereby when their submarine had been completely disabled, incapacitated, they would blow it up themselves, and that's what happened to this one. For a long time I had a piece of deck planking I had carried around from this particular boat.

---
*Destroyers Newcomb (DD-586) and Chandler (DD-206) sank the submarine I-185 on 22 June 1944.

Q: Rather than have to surface and be taken prisoner, they would destroy themselves?

Admiral Libby: Oh, yes. They'd just destroy the boat themselves. It's gruesome, but that's what they always did. It was rather, I thought, coincidental that my alarm and the reality thereof should happen almost simultaneously. After the Marianas "Turkey Shoot" was over, we went back to reestablish our position at Garapan Harbor on the west coast of Saipan. That's where we made the initial landings-- Tanapag Harbor, Garapan Harbor, and whatnot. After Saipan was pretty well occupied, holed-up Japs would be found from time to time; the last Japs were finally flushed out not too long ago. Tinian was just to the south, of course, and Tinian is much flatter. Tinian is nowhere near as mountainous as Saipan. They made a feint landing, a false landing, down on the west coast somewhere. The actual landing took place right across from Saipan on the north end of the island. Most of the ammunition fired at Tinian was Japanese ammunition captured on Saipan. It fit our guns all right.

Q: They were close enough so you could shoot from one island to the other.

Admiral Libby: They were Army stuff. I'm not talking about the Navy. They just shot it across. The occupation of Tinian was a pretty straightforward operation. It proceeded and just pushed them right off the south end of the island into the sea. They chose to die rather than surrender.

Q: Could you observe any of that from where you were?

Admiral Libby: Good Lord, yes. One fire support mission we had on the southeast tip of Tinian, just about the end of the show, was absolutely sickening. You could see these Japs just crowded up on the end like flies and we'd lob shells up in there.

Q: Did they walk into the ocean or just stay to be killed?

Admiral Libby: A little bit of both. This particular tip end was a cliff almost straight down, and most of them just stayed up there.

Q: Until the shells came?

Admiral Libby: Yes.

Q: That must have been a terrible emotional experience, or were you hardened to it by that time?

Admiral Libby: Yes. It wasn't pleasant. Anything about war is not pleasant anyway. And we weren't overly fond of the Japs about this point anyway. They were not regarded with favor. But that was pretty brutal.

Q: Could they have surrendered?

Admiral Libby: Sure, but they didn't. They never surrendered except when the Emperor told them to, finally, when war was over. Of course, that was what worried General Marshall, you know.* He absolutely insisted that we get Russia to come into the war. He was convinced that the Kwantung Army would not surrender.

Here's a good example of how the Japs play possum. There was a Japanese gun somewhere on the west coast of Tinian. Everybody knew where it was; we used to go down and take a free crack at it every now and then. We used to dust up Tinian, a little Saturday afternoon picnic. A couple of us would be sent down there to lob a few shells into Tinian just to let the Japs know that we had them on the agenda. We always threw a few shells in the general direction of this 5-inch gun--we knew roughly where it was dug in the mountains up there. After having disclosed its presence early in the game, they never peeped again for weeks, months. One fine afternoon, one of the battleships was down there and one of the destroyers. The battleship was anchored and lobbing shells at Tinian, and the destroyer was fortunately under way. All of a sudden, this gun opened fire--as I say, there had been no sign of life around that thing for weeks--and bang, just shot the daylights out of the destroyer, ruined the bridge,

---
*General George C. Marshall, U.S. Army, Chief of Staff of the Army throughout World War II.

killed the skipper, and raised hell generally with this destroyer, and made two or three hits in the battleship, which I believe was the Colorado. They finally succeeded in getting it to shut up again, because I think the Colorado fired a few big shells at it. They really raised hell with that destroyer. This destroyer had had rough luck anyway.* But that's what the Japs did. They'd play possum, and dig in, and then when you thought everything was hunky-dory, it turned out it wasn't.

The occupation of Tinian was a pretty routine show. It was a matter of putting additional force at the north end and walking south, is about what it amounted to. Tinian, of course, was on the agenda, because it's where we built the airfields for the B-17s that used to raid Japan from Tinian. Tinian was where the "Enola Gay" took off with the first nuclear bomb that bombed Hiroshima.** The whole north end of Tinian was mostly sugar cane and very flat and an ideal place to build airstrips. As I recall it, the capture of Guam took place while we were still involved in the Saipan-Tinian operation. This was sort of contemporaneous--a little bit later, but it overlapped. That

---

*On the morning of 24 July 1944, the day of the Tinian landings, the Norman Scott (DD-690) was bombarding from a position 1,800 yards from the shoreline. The Colorado (BB-45) was about 3,000 yards offshore. Within 15 minutes after the Japanese shore battery opened fire, it scored six hits on the Norman Scott, killed 19 men--including the commanding officer, Commander Seymour D. Owens, USN--and wounded 47. The ship sustained considerable damage. The Colorado was hit 22 times and received heavy casualties among topside personnel--43 killed and 97 wounded. See Samuel Eliot Morison, New Guinea and the Marianas (Boston: Little, Brown, 1953), pages 361-362.

**On 6 August 1945, a B-29 bomber nicknamed "Enola Gay" flew from Tinian to Hiroshima, Japan, on a mission which involved the first combat use of an atomic bomb.

was started before the Saipan-Tinian show was over. I wasn't down at Guam.

I remember that the first Marines on Guam were greeted with a great big sign on the beach that said, "Welcome, Marines. You are landing with the courtesy of the 204th Underwater Demolition Team."

We were in and around the Marianas for quite a while and found a great many amusing anecdotes and a great many amusing memories. One time there had been a typhoon off to the west of us, and we had a very heavy ground swell coming in from the west. And then there was a little blow down south, and we had a good strong south wind blowing. The combination of the south wind and the ground swell from the west broke the ocean up into squares just like a checker board.

Q: Could you see it?

Admiral Libby: You certainly could. The ground swells coming in from the west and the wind waves coming up from the south--it just broke the ocean up into a checkerboard.

Q: Had you ever seen that before?

Admiral Libby: No, and I've never seen it since. It takes an absolutely perfect combination of effect--the wind from due south, and the swell from due west. One of the most spectacular things out there were the sunsets. The air being full of smoke and dust, and everything, from all the bombardment on the island, great clouds of dust would get in the upper atmosphere and then at night you'd have tremendous refraction of the sun's rays, and you'd have the big white clouds--absolutely spectacularly beautiful sunsets. I've never seen the like of it before or since.

Q: Enormous cloud formations, I'm sure.

Admiral Libby: Yes, every night. We just used to look forward to seeing it. It was a beautiful display. One little side effect--there was a black cow that apparently had belonged to the natives who lived up on the hill in back of Garapan Harbor. That black cow was thin and scrawny but paid no attention to gunfire, bombs, napalm, and stuff all around her, over her, and underneath her. She just paid no attention to it all, as if to say these humans are certainly crazy. She was finally liberated by the Marines, and I believe that she became beefsteak, but I'm not sure. She certainly went through it and never paid the slightest attention to any of the sound and the fury around her.

Another little episode of some interest--the Japanese had a couple of guns, about 8 inch, right on the southern end of Saipan in concrete encasements with a little slit about so high out of which they could shoot. The USS *Tennessee*, in a pre-landing shore bombardment, pre-D-Day bombardment, put a 14-inch shell right down the muzzle of one of these guns. A direct hit right in the muzzle of one of these guns. Purely fortuitous but quite spectacular.

Q: Could you see it blow up?

Admiral Libby: I wasn't there. We were up at the northern end of the island when this took place. We almost had a delay in the Marianas show, because they were loading a lot of the LSTs over in West Loch, in Pearl Harbor. This took place on a Sunday afternoon. They were loading ammunition on some of these LSTs and somebody dropped a 5-inch shell, or something, and it went off and we burned up about 12 or 15 LSTs--had one hell of a fire over there.* It almost delayed the operation, but they decided to get along with what they had.

To get the idea of the meticulous planning involved--some of these landing craft and some of the LCVPs, and that sort of thing, top speed about eight knots, or ten knots, maybe, took off in great caravans weeks before the large ships did and strewed out across the ocean. We all arrived there at the same time the morning of the landing, but it was quite a chore. Admiral Turner's staff knew their stuff. They had some of the most competent people on it that have ever been assembled, I think. People like Jack Taylor.** I have the highest admiration for them; they really knew their stuff. Even when things were getting a little tense, Admiral Turner was always calm as a cucumber. The

---
*Six LSTs and three LCTs were lost; casualties amounted to 163 dead and 396 injured. See Samuel Eliot Morison, New Guinea and the Marianas (Boston: Little, Brown, 1953), page 171.
**Commander John McN. Taylor, USN, was Turner's staff gunnery officer.

highest tribute I can pay that man is the fact that you always knew exactly what he wanted you to do, and that's a big help. Sometimes he would tell you rather emphatically what he wanted you to do, but you knew.

Q: I don't think the person who wants to do the job right is offended as long as the man tells you. I don't care how he tells you, as long as you know if you do it he'll back you up.

Admiral Libby: Sure. Well, one afternoon when the island had been pretty well occupied, the Marines decided it was safe for some of the sailors to come ashore. I was invited to go ashore one afternoon and bring Larry Cook and some of my destroyer people with me so that the Marines could take us up and show us what we had achieved with our destroyer gunfire support. We went up in a jeep, and the jeep had a couple of riflemen riding pillion on it in case any Japs decided to have at us. The company commander was with us, and we came to one cave there and the company commander turned to this little boy who looked to me to be about 14 years old. I don't think he had ever shaved in his life. He didn't look it anyway--baby-faced Marine. The captain said, "Tell them what happened to you up here."

The boy said, "Well, Sir, I went up to this cave and I lobbed a grenade in there and I said, 'Come on out,' and 18 of them came out. I thought they never would stop coming out. Boy, they just scared the hell out of me." He had captured 18 Japs--this little boy all by himself.

Q: That was a case where they did surrender.

Admiral Libby: They did in driblets. By this time, all their officers had been killed or committed hara-kari. There were just the remnants left, and most of them didn't know what the score was. They had been pretty well shocked and shot up.

Sometime I hope somebody will take a computer and figure out how many tons of metal and high explosive it takes to kill one man in a big war. It's an awful lot. If you'd divide the number of men killed into the pounds of powder and shell and shot that had been expended, it takes a lot of stuff to kill a man.

Libby #3 - 131

Interview Number 3 with Vice Admiral Ruthven E. Libby, U.S. Navy (Retired)

Place: Admiral Libby's home, Coronado, California

Date: 10 May 1970

Subject: Biography

Interviewer: Commander Etta-Belle Kitchen, U.S. Navy (Retired)

Q: We left, Admiral, at the end of Saipan and Tinian, and we're going to go to the period where you were in the southern Palau Islands. I wish you would tell me the task force and the names of the people involved and all the detail that you can recall in connection with that operation.

Admiral Libby: When we got sprung from the Marianas operation, I took my destroyer squadron down south and we joined up with Admiral Ainsworth, who had a cruiser division, and Admiral Hayler, who had another cruiser division.* We spent about a week or ten days at Iron Bottom Bay there at Tulagi while the plans for the Palau operation were being finalized. Then we took off with Admiral Ainsworth and Admiral Hayler and my squadron of destroyers, and another squadron, I think. We went down to Guadalcanal where we rehearsed the operation, the amphibious operation, for the landing at Pelelieu and Angaur. Rear Admiral George Fort was in command of the overall command; his chief of staff was Benny Decker; his gunnery officer was Bruce

---
*Rear Admiral Walden L. Ainsworth, USN; Rear Admiral Robert W. Hayler, USN.

Kelley.* Part of the force was Admiral Oldendorf and his battleships.** As I say, Ainsworth and Bob Hayler had their cruiser divisions, and I had my own Destroyer Squadron 56 and several other minor ships of various sorts and shapes. I had the overall screen. That was my job, to screen the operation against submarines and whatnot--similar to what I had had up in the Marianas.

Of course, the usual submarine reconnaissance had been made at Pelelieu-Angaur. It had been decided to bypass Babelthuap, which was the biggest island. It had the number one Japanese garrison, but it had been determined that if we could get Pelelieu and Angaur, we could put in an airfield on Angaur. As a matter of fact, the topography of Saipan, Tinian, and Pelelieu-Angaur were rather similar. Saipan was mountainous and large, and Tinian was close by and flat. Pelelieu was mountainous and fairly large, and Angaur was a southern adjunct and flat, separated by a very narrow waterway between the two islands. The main reason we wanted Angaur was to put a B-17 bomber field on it--for what purpose I don't really know, but that was the idea.

Q: All of this was in preparation for the Philippines operation.

Admiral Libby: That's right. It was in preparation for the Leyte Gulf landing in the Philippines--one step up toward that general area. We went down there for the pre-D-Day bombardment, and the first night

---

*Commander Bruce D. Kelley, USN.
**Rear Admiral Jesse B. Oldendorf, USN.

the whole fleet assembled--the amphibious outfit and whatnot--somebody had the idea that the small ships should retire to the eastward of Pelelieu at night, and the big ships should come around to the westward. Who dreamed this one up, I don't know, but that first night was pretty grim, because the passageway between the two islands wasn't any bigger than the top of this table, and we had half of one fleet trying to go west through this thing on a pitch-black night, darken ship, and the other half trying to go east through this thing. It was not such a hot operation; somebody thought better of that, and it never happened again. After that, if it was decided we had to shift station, we did it before night fell. That was just one of the many amusing things that happened during this operation.

Q: Did you want to go into any detail about your experience down in Guadalcanal?

Admiral Libby: That was no experience at all. We never got ashore there. We were simply anchored off there. We used Guadalcanal as a practice target; the island had long since been in American hands. We simply used it as a target for the rehearsal for the amphibious operation landing on Pelelieu. It was a fairly routine rehearsal. Nothing untoward happened at all.

Q: What date was it that you went up to Pelelieu?

Libby #3 - 134

Admiral Libby: I think we first got up there about the 12th of September, if I recollect correctly, and the landing actually took place on the 15th, after the usual pre-D-Day bombardments. The reconnaissance at Pelelieu was not too thorough. It was as thorough as we knew how to make it with submarine photographs, aerial photographs, and what not, but it fooled everybody. It turned out to be an extremely difficult terrain, which nobody realized. It looked from seaward and from the air just like an ordinary South Pacific island, more or less covered with trees and the usual, but what actually turned out, except for the very southern end, it was very much, instead of being an ordinary island, like a loaf of pre-sliced bread--a whole series of pinnacles and peaks and steep declivities and valleys from the south up to the north, and so covered with vegetation that nobody had any real conception of the terrain. It turned out to be a very costly thing to take--full of caves and full of declivities, and we had to fight every inch of the way. It was a vicious island to capture, horrible. Of course, the Japs were masters at digging in, you know, and they were all in caves.

The poor people on the beach had a hell of a time. We gave them all the gunfire support we could, controlled gunfire support. The people at sea did everything they possibly could to help them, but it was a pretty tough operation on the beach. One thing that happened-- we had some white phosphorus shells, 5-inch, aboard the Newcomb, as I remember. This white phosphorus shell is a very useful shell for incendiary purposes and also for spotting. It puts up a good cloud of white smoke and is a very good indicator where you want bombs dropped, or something. It also is particularly useful is you want to start a fire; it's very hot stuff. We had some of these shells, and we used to try to fire them at a very high elevation, because we were close in to shore and to get up to the height that we had to have, we had to fire them just about straight up, almost vertical. We also had to fire reduced charge, because the thing weighed practically nothing; it's a very light shell, and if you put in a full powder charge it would overshoot the target. We found, to our consternation, that with a reduced powder charge there wasn't sufficient setback to arm the projectile, and nothing would happen. An ordinary naval projectile is armed by what they call a setback--the initial acceleration of the shell arms the fuze. That keeps it from going off if someone drops it. We had to get the Bureau of Ordnance to change the setback on these things completely.

This operation dragged on for some time, a long, long time. It started the 15th of September, and I think the whole thing was contained (by that I mean the Japanese reinforcements that used to come down every night by barge were shut off) by a matter of a week or ten days after the initial landing. But it was another month before the thing was finally cleaned up and finally reduced. We used to go to Kossol Roads to rearm and reammunition our ships and then go back down. The destroyers' principal job there, as it was at Saipan, was gunfire support, star shell firing at night to keep the Japs up all night, and whatnot. We did an awful lot of gunfiring, but there were

Libby #3 - 136

only one or two skirmishes with some of these barges that the Japs brought down.

I remember one of my destroyer skippers, Jock Cooper, who had the <u>Bennion</u>.* We were on the east side of Pelelieu one night about 1:00 a.m., and Jock got on the TBS and said there were about 15 or 20 Japanese landing barges coming down loaded with troops.** We sent a couple, three, destroyers up, and they disposed of these people neatly and tidily, but in order to find out where he was I said, "What is your location?"

And he came back and said, "I'm eight miles due east of unpronounceable island." I knew exactly where he was. The names of these islands were really out of this world. One of the more pronounceable ones was Babelthuap, but nobody could pronounce this one.

Our part of the operation, from the viewpoint of those of us at sea, was very unspectacular and very routine and a little bit on the boring side. We never had any attack from Japanese air, Japanese submarines, or anything else out there. Of course, the Japs' fleet had been pretty well emasculated by then anyway, but there was the usual business of trying to help out the people on the beach, and they really caught hell at this Palau operation. It was a vicious thing because of how terrible the terrain turned out to be, which nobody had any concept of. We would blow all the vegetation off and find just a series of hog-back ridges running like a loaf of pre-sliced bread.

*Commander Joshua W. Cooper, USN.
**TBS---talk between ships---voice radio.

Libby #3 - 137

Q: Some of the historians say that this was one of Admiral Nimitz's mistakes—that we didn't need to take this island at all.

Admiral Libby: I don't agree at all. I think we did need to take it. I will rise to remark at this particular point that whatever the historians may say, with whatever benefit of Monday morning quarterbacking, I think that between Admiral King and Admiral Nimitz and "Savvy" Cooke, Admiral King's chief planner back in Washington, their selection of what points in the Pacific to assault, and what points to bypass, amounted to nothing short of genius.* If you look back at those that we did take—they were every one of them a node in the whole Japanese nervous system of their Pacific occupation. Every time one of those islands was pinched off, thousands and thousands of Japanese died on the vine. They were just abandoned and literally died on the vine. If we had adopted the war plan which sat in the archives of the Navy Department from the end of World War I, the Orange war plan, we would never have gotten beyond Pearl Harbor.** I say the island-hopping technique which Admiral King, Admiral Nimitz, and "Savvy" Cooke worked out between themselves, was absolutely

---

*Admiral Ernest J. King, USN, Commander in Chief U.S. Fleet; Admiral Chester W. Nimitz, USN, Commander in Chief Pacific Fleet and Pacific Ocean Areas; Vice Admiral Charles M. Cooke, Jr., USN, who held a number of titles in succession: Assistant Chief of Staff (Plans), Deputy Chief of Staff, and finally Chief of Staff.
**In the plans contemplated between World Wars, the U.S. battleships were to steam west and have a battle against the Japanese fleet in the vicinity of the Marshall Islands. With the battleships largely put out of action in the attack on Pearl Harbor, a new plan was needed. Orange was the code name for Japan in the prewar plans.

genius.

Look at the record. Look at what happened. If you can point out to me that was a mistake--I don't think Pelelieu-Angaur was at all. I just don't believe it. There are millions of islands out there; the Japs had completely unrestricted sway from the end of World War I, when they got the mandate, until Pearl Harbor, and long after that, as a matter of fact. They picked out the key points; they fortified them; they knew them like they knew the back of their hands, as we found out. We didn't. They could run around in the middle of the night. They knew; we didn't know where the hell we were. That's why we got the hell beat out of us at Savo and some of those early battles--we didn't know where we were.* We didn't have any charts; we didn't know the terrain; we just weren't prepared to fight in those waters and the Japs were. Had we tried to form a cordon and just push across and have a great front line across the South Pacific, we never would have gotten to first base.

I remember when Admiral King ordered the assault on Guadalcanal from Washington. He was one of the handful of people in the Navy who ever heard of Guadalcanal. I'd never heard of it; I didn't know where the hell it was; it meant nothing to me, and I couldn't figure what it was all about. I couldn't figure out why. He sent Admiral Turner down with a pitifully unprepared outfit. We didn't know anything about amphibious warfare in those days. That was Richmond Kelly

---

*Savo refers to the Japanese sinking of four Allied cruisers in the vicinity of Guadalcanal and Savo Island the night of 8-9 August 1942.

Turner's really first tough assignment. He could have taken an awful licking.* As it turned out, we lost an awful lot of ships at first Savo but the Japanese didn't come on in and attack the transports. They turned around and went back. Thank God, the Japs make mistakes, too. The reaction of the Japanese to our assault on Guadalcanal was really something, and that really started it. They threw everything they had to try to chase us out of there. That was proof enough to me that Admiral King knew exactly what a sensitive spot it was. He decided he would make a stand there, and that would save Australia, and it did. What genius enabled him to pick Guadalcanal out of the blue I don't know, but he did. That's why I say we are blessed to have people with brains in this country when we need them. Up until now. At the moment, I don't know. But we had then.

Q: Today is another situation.

Admiral Libby: And because then, also, patriotism was not a dirty word. The kids knew what it was all about and were ready, able, and willing to fight for their country. I simply don't agree that Pelelieu-Angaur was a mistake on Admiral Nimitz's part at all.

Q: History says, also, that the Japanese started a different type of defensive operation on this island which was responsible for a heavy loss of life.

---
*Rear Admiral Richmond Kelly Turner, USN, commander of the amphibious task force at Guadalcanal.

Admiral Libby: I don't agree with that either. The terrain of the island was, as I say, something that none of us suspected, I'm sure. We sailed up to it three or four days before landing and did our preliminary bombardment and supported the underwater demolition team--- it looked just like another island to us.

Q: Just like one hill?

Admiral Libby: Just like a loaf of bread---a usual, handsome, South Pacific island with trees all over it with no indication of what it really was like. The Japs had dug into every cave and took advantage of every bit of terrain, and they were really prepared. It was a rough thing to drive them out.

Q: It was really defense in tremendous depth then?

Admiral Libby: Absolutely. There wasn't anything new about it. The Japs were absolutely marvelous at underground digging in, using caves, and stuff of that sort. There wasn't anything out of the ordinary about it, except the very rugged terrain the poor devils had to fight.

Q: Do you recall if this was the first time we used flame throwers?

Admiral Libby: Heavens, no. They were one of the standard weapons, as far as I know, all through the war. I've seen them used on Saipan and Tinian. I don't think it was the first time they were used at all. Of course, Angaur was like shooting fish in a rain barrel. After Pelelieu, Angaur was flat. We just walked in and took it over. We didn't have any real difficulty there.

When that was all over, I think we got sprung about the middle of October, we went up to Manus and anchored there. I turned my squadron over to Commodore Roland Nesbit Smoot (now Vice Admiral), who now lives up in Leisure World.* He's a man you ought to talk to. I turned my squadron over to him and went back to Washington and Roland had the privilege of taking the squadron through the Surigao Strait battle, which I missed by about a week.

Q: You received your second and third Gold Star in lieu of a second and third Legion of Merit and the ship, the <u>Newcomb</u>, received the Navy Unit Commendation for her actions.

Admiral Libby: I wouldn't be surprised. She was a good ship. I think she probably got that for Surigao Strait, didn't she?

Q: She received it for outstanding heroism and action against enemy Japanese forces in the Saipan-Tinian operations, May 29 to August 5; Palau, September 6 to October 1; and the battle of Surigao Strait, October 24-25. I believe you said you went to the planning section of

---

*Vice Admiral Roland Nesbit Smoot, USN (Ret.), whose oral history is in the Naval Institute collection.

Libby #3 - 142

CNO.

Admiral Libby: That was after the war. I went back after Pelelieu-Angaur. I was detached and flew back to Washington and became the senior Navy member of the Joint War Plans Committee. My contemporaries, my opposite numbers were Bill Bessell, brigadier general in the Army, and Frank Everest who was a brigadier general in the Army Air Corps, later to become the Air Force.* In order that I could breathe down the backs of these two brigadier generals, I was given the dubious honor of being promoted to commodore, one star.

I was summoned to Admiral King's office to be sworn in as commodore. I said, "Admiral, I don't know whether this is the kiss of death or it means that I have one foot in the door." He laughed heartily, and I became a commodore. The three of us ran the Joint War Plans Committee from then until I was detached in February, '46.

Q: So you had rather a long period of duty there in CNO going from one duty to the other, and I'm sure many interesting things happened in that time.

Admiral Libby: Most of it was with the War Plans Committee. This business you asked about the 38th parallel in Korea--along about the middle of July, '45, we were meeting then in what was then the new

---

*Brigadier General William W. Bessell, Jr., U.S. Army; Brigadier General Frank F. Everest, Jr., U.S. Army.

Libby #3 - 143

State Department Building, 23rd and Virginia. Now it's one of the horde of State Department buildings that they have around town, but then it was brand spanking new. We had the second deck up there.

It had become quite apparent that V-J Day was not far off. This was after the Russians had entered the war, so it was after Hiroshima and Nagasaki. We knew the Japanese were about to surrender and V-J Day was not far off. This was about 2:00 o'clock in the afternoon, and Bill Bessell went over and hauled down a roller map (like a window shade) of the Korean Peninsula, and he said, "Now look." He took a pointer and drew a line across it. He said, "Let's have the Russians take the Japanese surrender north of the 38th parallel and we'll take it south of the 38th parallel." A matter of convenience, logistics, and that's all the thought ever was given to it. The Chiefs just said okay, and that's what produced the 38th parallel at Korea--just like that. Nobody realized, of course, except the Joint Strategic Survey Committee, who had written a paper sometime before. Nobody stopped to realize--I know that Marshall and King and company knew, but they had never thought it politic to mention it from a political viewpoint that the Russians were anything but our friends. I don't think any of them had any conception of what kind of people they really were. Nobody stopped to think that all the brains and energy, and all the power plants and everything in Korea was north of the 38th parallel and that south of it was just rice paddies and peasants, even though the capital, Seoul, was south of it. All the zing was really north of the 38th parallel.

Libby #3 - 144

To interject--this I can't prove, but I don't think I dreamed this. There was an organization which Admiral King set up, urged it be set up, about 18 months before the war was over, called the Joint Strategic Survey Committee. Admiral Russell Willson was our Navy member, and we had an Army member and an Army Air Corps member.*

Q: Captain Rochefort served on that committee.**

Admiral Libby: We used to call them the "Stratospheric Thinkers," and their job was to look ahead as far as they could and not be concerned with day-to-day nuts and bolts of the war but to look ahead and take the broad gauge view and recommend. I will swear that they wrote a paper and handed it to the Joint Chiefs of Staff which said, in effect, V-J Day is not far away. We have now produced the greatest military machine that the world has ever seen, and the minute the Japs surrender the thing to do is turn the guns 180 degrees, point them right down Joe Stalin's throat and say, "Joe, sign here or else." I will swear that that paper was written and presented to the Joint Chiefs of Staff, but I can't prove it. And, of course, the Joint Chiefs of Staff laughed politely and threw it in the wastebasket. It was politically impossible; you can imagine what would have happened. I don't think I dreamed that up myself.

---
*Rear Admiral Russell Willson, USN.
**Captain Joseph J. Rochefort, USN, whose oral history is in the Naval Institute collection.

Libby #3 - 145

Q: But it would still be in existence.

Admiral Libby: I don't know. This was 25 years ago.

Q: And there were some very farsighted people on that committee.

Admiral Libby: That was 25 years ago, but I will swear that that paper was written, and it showed up in a Joint Chiefs of Staff meeting. As I say, the Joint Chiefs laughed politely and gave it the deep six, because there was nothing else they could do. If I haven't invented the whole thing, it never got beyond that meeting. It probably is still in the archives somewhere, and it would be interesting to look it up and see what it says. It certainly would have made sense if we had done it. All our troubles would be over today.

Q: You don't know why Bessell said 38th parallel?

Admiral Libby: It was convenient. It was halfway up.

Q: It looked like a good division on the map?

Admiral Libby: It looked like a good geographical division—that's all there was to it. The Russians were already up there. We were down south then; we would have to go up there. It was a convenient whack-up; it cut the country roughly in half. Give the Russians the northern half, us the southern half. That's all anybody thought about.

Q: We were very generous in those days.

Admiral Libby: Oh, sure. It never occurred to us that they would just stay. We thought they would take the Japanese surrender and go home, naive us.

Q: Like we did in Japan.

Admiral Libby: Naive us. Just as Eisenhower was ordered to let the Russians get into Berlin first, because after the war the Germans would hate the Russians worse than they hated us.* That was the logic of that. We're very naive at times.

Q: I'm sure there were other things that you considered during that period when you were the senior member of the War Plans Committee.

Admiral Libby: The nuts and bolts, and the day-to-day work. I remember we were busily engaged in planning for the invasion of Kyushu which, fortunately, never had to take place. The first steps of the

---

*General of the Army Dwight D. Eisenhower, Supreme Commander Allied Expeditionary Force.

Libby #3 - 147

operation had already been set in motion--it takes a long time to get one of these big operations going--before Hiroshima. But we figured there would be--we picked a nice round number of one million casualties from the invasion of Kyushu. I didn't mean one million people killed but killed and wounded. I think it would have been low, because judging from the fanatical way in which the Japanese fought--and this being an invasion of their homeland--it would have been horrible. Thank God, it never took place. Whatever the virtues or sins of nuclear weapons, they saved an awful lot of lives during World War II.

Q: At one time you said that General Marshall believed that Japan would never surrender.* Did that have anything to do with any of your plans?

Admiral Libby: Not directly. General Marshall's conviction that we absolutely had to get the Russians to come into the war didn't affect our work particularly, because it was above our level. We never had to plan any joint action with the Soviets or anything of that sort. In my opinion, General Marshall's conviction that the Russians had to come in cost us mainland China--it was a terrific mistake.

Q: Incalculable.

---
*General of the Army George C. Marshall, Chief of Staff, U.S. Army, throughout the war.

Admiral Libby: It was a perfectly honest mistake. He believed it firmly, and any man that operates on a high level that he did, then and subsequently, when he makes a mistake it's a dilly. I never felt that he was in any way to be censured for this. He was just mistaken, that's all. It was a terrifically expensive mistake, I think, and it's too bad. The whole thing was a culmination of bad advice that Roosevelt got and his conviction that he could handle Joe Stalin. Russia never should have been allowed to get into the Pacific war at all, because she contributed nothing; they had no need of her, and we paid a horrible price for it. Marshall was convinced that the Kwantung Army, which was all over north China, would not obey the Emperor's instructions to surrender--that they would just keep on fighting. Of course, the minute the Emperor said, "That's it, boys," they all quit, just like that. Naturally, what hindsight says they would do. Marshall's subsequent efforts to get Gimo and Chou En-lai in bed together after the war didn't work, but on that one he was just being a good soldier.* He was just doing what Harry Truman wanted him to do. He did what he was told. He contributed to the loss of the mainland China to the communists, but he was not responsible for it. The people responsible for it were others--Harry Dexter White, Currie,

---

*Chou En-lai--Chinese Communist leader second to Mao Tse-Tung by the end of World War II; later Premier of the People's Republic. Gimo is a nickname for Generalissimo Chiang Kai-shek of Nationalist China.

Libby #3 - 149

and all that gang.*

Q: In the State Department?

Admiral Libby: Yes. I can't think of any other outstanding developments while I was back in Washington on the Joint War Plans Committee.

Q: It was an extremely important era, however, in which many important things were taking place.

Admiral Libby: Oh, yes. Things were grinding around at a great rate. I do remember that we used to get briefed every morning, see what was going on in Europe, and whatnot. We saw the Battle of the Bulge developing and wondered why nobody did anything about it.**

Q: Can you expand on that?

Admiral Libby: I just remember that it was perfectly obvious to us in

---
*Harry Dexter White, Assistant Secretary of the Treasury under Truman, accused of being a Communist spy. No proof was ever found. Lauchlin Currie, a member of the State Department whose name was included in testimony given by Elizabeth Bentley and Whittaker Chambers before a New York grand jury concerning infiltration of "communists."
**The Battle of the Bulge was a German counteroffensive in the semimountainous Ardennes region of Belgium and Luxembourg in December 1944, so called because of the bulge the attack created in the American lines. It was a considerable surprise to the Allied forces, because Germany was considered essentially defeated by then.

Libby #3 - 150

Washington that this was going to happen, but nobody saw fit to do anything about it over in Europe, apparently. Why, I've never known. That's beyond the scope of this book. I wasn't there; I don't know. I just remember that a lot of us were surprised that nothing, no steps were taken to counter it in time. Of course, everybody was busy and everybody was preoccupied, and I suppose everybody had other things to do. Maybe they figured that was the best thing to do, to let them break through and seal them off from there, but it looked very odd to us.

Q: How did you function? You were briefed each morning by someone from the JCS?*

Admiral Libby: Everybody went around to a briefing by the Joint Intelligence Committee, JIC, and they briefed the Joint Chiefs and all of us lesser lights every morning. It was perfectly routine. It's probably going on today--everybody going down to get the dope on what's going on. It was just a normal briefing.

Q: And then you go back and try to come to some evaluation and write a paper and present it to JCS?

Admiral Libby: This was just part of the grist for our mill, just the general information that we got to work from. We didn't have to take

---
*JCS--Joint Chiefs of Staff.

Libby #3 - 151

any specific action on it particularly, unless it affected what we were up to that moment.

Q: When you had a recommendation, did you put it in the form of a paper?

Admiral Libby: Oh, sure. Europe was not our bailiwick at that point. We were not concerned with it. We didn't make plans for tactical operations in the field. What we wrote there were the strategic plans. Europe had passed the point that the Joint War Plans Committee would be involved in it.

Q: Your information was to go to JCS for their actions?

Admiral Libby: That's right. Europe at that point was the responsibility of the Europeans, the people over there. The war plans had long since been made. They were just fighting the thing from day to day.

Q: So you were detached from JCS.

Admiral Libby: I was detached from Admiral King's staff and ordered out to command Cruiser Division 11; it was supposed to be a division of four antiaircraft cruisers. I arrived out here in February or March of '46 and reported aboard the Tucson, one of the light

antiaircraft cruisers. Harry Sanders had command of it at the time.*
I hoisted my one-star flag proudly out here and went over to call on
the local command. Then I went up to Long Beach to call on the
admiral up there who had cruisers on the West Coast. I walked into
the St. Paul and was greeted by the admiral's chief of staff who said,
"Haven't you seen dispatch thus and so?"

I said, no, I hadn't, so he dug it out of his files and it said,
"Cruiser Division 11 dissolved." So there I was, dissolved.

Q: That's what they mean by brief duty.

Admiral Libby: Four days after assuming command I was dissolved. I
was delighted really. I called up Roland Smoot, chief of officer
detail in BuPers, and said, "What do I do now?"**

He said, "What do you mean what do you do now?"

I said, "Haven't you seen BuPers dispatch thus and so?"

He said, "No, I haven't."

I said, "Maybe you'd better look it up."

So he said, "Wait a minute."

He picked up the phone then said, "Jesus Christ. I'll call you
back." Then ensued a certain amount of pelekea, after which I was
told (A) that I was no longer a commodore; I had reverted to four
stripes, captain's stripes, which delighted my soul. I was much

---

*Captain Harry Sanders, USN, who, coincidentally, like Libby, was a member of Admiral King's staff at the beginning of the war.
**BuPers—Bureau of Naval Personnel.

happier as a captain than I had ever been as a commodore. Then I was offered command of the USS Kentucky, which was a battleship about three-quarters completed. I said, "Thank you very much. If there's anything that floats, I'd rather have something that floats." So I was given command of the Bremerton, which was then in Shanghai. The Kentucky never was completed, as you know, so if I had taken command of the Kentucky, I never would have had a deep-draft command.*

I got aboard a transport and rode for 21 days nonstop and arrived in Shanghai and took command of the Bremerton and spent a very pleasant year out there in the western Pacific. I brought her back and took her into the Bremerton Navy Yard for overhaul and then went out and reported to Louie Denfeld's staff in Pearl Harbor.**

Q: What was Shanghai like in '46?

Admiral Libby: We didn't spend much time in Shanghai; we were in and out; we were up and down. We went down to Hong Kong and up to Tsingtao and all around. We covered Guam, Saipan, Tinian. We covered the Western Pacific pretty thoroughly. Shanghai was bustling and, of course, all the mainland of China was in the throes of an appalling inflation. Something that people ought to give some heed to right here in this country today is that the number one weapon, if you want to destroy a country, is to inflate their currency. I have somewhere

---
*Construction of the Kentucky wound up being suspended in February 1947, when she was about 70% complete.
**Admiral Louis E. Denfeld, USN, Commander in Chief Pacific Fleet.

in my archives a bill for a dinner that I gave in Shanghai, at the French Club one night, for three people and myself. It was the simplest dinner you can imagine—a little bit of meat, a boiled potato, a piece of bread, a little salad, and one bottle of wine, something of that order. There wasn't much food there anyway in those days. We didn't have any cocktails; we had those at my suite at the Cathay Hotel beforehand. The bill for that dinner was 33 million—33 million Chinese dollars.

There was an old gal who sat on the steps of the Cathay Hotel and sold newspapers. I have said this many times. I have seen somebody buy a newspaper from her and give her more money for the paper than there was paper in the newspaper—just bales of this stuff. It was completely worthless, but it was all the poor devils had. Of course, this was one jump ahead of their hightailing it for Taiwan.

You can see the same thing going on in this country today, the same process going on today that went on in China, went on everywhere else. You debase the currency, you fill the kids full of drugs, you infiltrate the schools. The same process is going on across the United States today, exactly. Inflation is just beginning in this country. Believe me, there isn't anything more vicious to completely destroy civilization than runaway inflation. You'll see it in this country inside the next couple of years, particularly if dear old Teddy gets in to be our President in 1972.[*]

---

[*] Edward M. "Ted" Kennedy.

Libby #3 - 155

Q: What was the mission of the Bremerton when she was out in Shanghai?

Admiral Libby: We were simply part of the Western Pacific Fleet. At the time we had a couple of carriers--the Princeton and the Tarawa. We had the Bremerton and the Toledo; then we had a couple of squadrons of destroyers, and we had a few amphibious ships. We were simply the WestPac United States Navy, which used to be the old Asiatic Fleet. We were showing the flag.

One job I had, I was sent down to Hong Kong. I spent a month down there and my job was to sort of sweep up--get the U.S. Navy out of Hong Kong after the war, including running down Turner Joy's golf clubs which he had left in the Peninsular Hotel.*

Q: In Hong Kong--before the war?

Admiral Libby: In Hong Kong, Kowloon, after the war. My job was to sweep up and get the remnants of the U.S. Navy out of the Hong Kong area, round up all the illegal jeeps, close up the remnants of the shore establishments we had around there, which we did. Nothing very spectacular about that but interesting.

Q: Any anecdotes about that that would be interesting?

---
*Rear Admiral Charles Turner Joy, USN.

Admiral Libby: There is one anecdote. We were moored to a buoy in Hong Kong Harbor with the beach here, a wreck here, and a wreck here--a triangle--wrecks fore and aft and the beach on one side and a little bit of open water on the other side. One fine morning, or rather, one un-fine morning, we had, not the wind, but the rain of the outskirts of a typhoon. It rained 22 inches in 11 hours. Believe me, the heavens just opened. If you've ever been in a typhoon, you know it really rains. At Repulse Bay and Hong Kong the mountains are very steep, and the wash set up these terrific currents in the harbor (the wash off the mountain with all this water running down). I was sitting in my cabin about 11:30 in the morning, and I had a compass dial in front of me. I noticed that the ship had swung 180 degrees plus 90 more in about 30 seconds--just swung around like that. Then I felt my cabin rise about three feet, and I rushed up on the bridge and discovered that we had snubbed our anchor chain across the bow and broken it. And there we were, free ballooning in Hong Kong Harbor with no steam up or anything else, which was a mistake on my part. I should have ordered steam up, but I never figured we'd break our anchor chain. Jesse Gay, who was my first lieutenant, hit the forecastle just about the time I hit the bridge, and I remember he had on shorts and tennis shoes--he had been taking his exercises--and he hit the wet deck and skidded, slid all the way up to the foreward capstan, grabbed a maul on his way by, and let go the other anchor.*
That saved us; otherwise, we would have been in embarrassing

---
*Commander Jesse B. Gay, Jr., USN.

circumstances.

Q: Real serious circumstances, I'm sure.

Admiral Libby: When things calmed down, Jesse, who was a terrific athlete, decided he would recover our anchor chain, so without benefit of helmet, he just dove down and found the anchor and tied a line to it and got it back up.

Q: It would seem almost a superhuman act.

Admiral Libby: It wasn't so much that as the fact that you don't go swimming in Chinese waters if you're smart--you just don't do it. So instead of giving him a medal, we gave him a big dose of salts to save his life. He came to no untoward end about this, thank God, but he could have gotten all kinds of stuff.

Q: Because of the filth in the water?

Admiral Libby: That's right. We'd been there for a month and had made a lot of friends among the British, of course. It is still a British crown colony. They had a four-star admiral and all sorts of dignitaries down there. The night before we left, I decided to give a cocktail party over at the hotel. Because we were getting under way at 8:00 a.m., I decided to get back to the ship at a reasonable hour.

Libby #3 - 158

I went back to the ship about 10:00 o'clock, but I instructed my gunnery officer to keep the bar open at the party as long as the British stayed. It was supposed to be a regular cocktail party from 6:00 until about 8:00 or 9:00, but I had heard that the British would stay as long as the bar remained open, so I said, "Let's try this out." My gunnery officer got home at 4:00 a.m. The last British were wrapped up and gone home just before 4:00 o'clock.

Ordinarily, I'm not very smart, but this particular time I had the wit to do something. I just had a hunch that something like this would happen. My gunnery officer paid the bill that night, and it was a good sizable bill. I said, "Be sure to get a receipted bill." He brought it back to the ship and I preserved it carefully, because I was absolutely certain that this would happen. Sure enough, about four months later I got a very indignant letter from the head of the hotel chain to which the Peninsular Hotel belonged--the Peninsular was over in Kowloon on the mainland side and, of course, headquarters were on Hong Kong Island. (Kowloon is on the mainland of China but is part of Hong Kong.) This letter had gone back to the Bureau of Personnel and finally caught up with me while I was in Honolulu on Louie Denfeld's staff, saying that I had jumped ship and hadn't paid my bill and would the Bureau of Personnel please take steps that this honorable bill be paid and not dishonored. Fortunately, I had the bill and I had photostatic copies by the dozen and I sent them all over the place. The next thing that happened I got a very apologetic letter from the hotel; but I just knew that what happened about it would happen.

Q: If you hadn't kept it, you would have been in bad shape.

Admiral Libby: Oh brother, yes. For some reason I just knew that would happen. Thank God, I had the stuff.

Q: What did you do with all the material that you rounded up in Hong Kong?

Admiral Libby: We sent it home. It wasn't really very much. We collected a few illegal jeeps and chased some of the old chiefs out who had been living happily ashore. We just wrapped up the odds and ends.

Q: That would probably make a story in itself, wouldn't it? The human interest?

Admiral Libby: I know I was very unpopular with all these people, if that's of any historical interest; people were having a very good time. They hated to be closed up. They didn't have much to do then. There are all kinds of activities that have to go on when you are supporting something, the logistic infrastructure, communication stations, service stations, and whatnot.

Libby #3 - 160

Q: How many chiefs did you have to break up housekeeping with?

Admiral Libby: Only three or four. Nothing very dramatic, but they were unhappy. After we got back, I was relieved up in Bremerton. I brought the Bremerton back to the Bremerton Navy Yard just before Christmas of '46.

Q: Then you went to work for Admiral Denfeld.

Admiral Libby: It was postwar, and there was nothing in any way spectacular about it at all. There was nothing that wasn't strictly routine. We were only out there a short while, less than a year, and about 11 months after that Admiral Denfeld became Chief of Naval Operations, and shortly thereafter I went back and got on his staff back in Washington.

Q: He went back before you?

Admiral Libby: He went back a couple of months before I did. There was nothing there that was in any way memorable at all; we just wound around the good old daily routine.

Q: What are your comments about Admiral Denfeld? Was he a good man to work for?

Admiral Libby: Very fine man, indeed.

Q: Did he ask for you to come back to Washington?

Admiral Libby: I presume so, otherwise I wouldn't have gone. I imagine he did. Admiral Denfeld was a very fine individual--is a very fine individual. I don't know why I speak of him in the past tense--he's very much alive.* His main problem when he became Chief of Naval Operations--that was just about the time of the National Security Act of 1947 and all that monkey business, and the so-called Revolt of the Admirals, all that kind of stuff, the grand era of Louis Johnson--horrible period, about as nightmarish an experience as I've ever lived through.**

Q: I'd like to have you describe that in as much detail as you can recall.

Admiral Libby: Let's put it this way. I'll try to be as dispassionate and objective as I can in light of what's happened. When the National Security Act of 1947 was initially passed and the Air Force sprang "full panoplied from the brow of Jove" like Minerva, as you know, Hoyt Vandenberg, who had been a chicken colonel up until

---
*Admiral Denfeld died in March 1972, almost two years after this interview was conducted.
**Louis A. Johnson assumed the position of Secretary of Defense when James V. Forrestal left in 1949.

that point, suddenly put on four stars and became Chief of Staff of the Air Force.* Our dear friend, W. Stuart Symington became Secretary of the Air Force.** Life in Washington suddenly became very difficult for the Navy. Between Stuart Symington and Hoyt Vandenberg (I think it must have been Stu Symington's idea, because Hoyt Vandenberg was too stupid to ever have an idea, in my humble opinion--De mortuis nil nisi bonum to the contrary, notwithstanding--I did not and do not and never will respect Hoyt Vandenberg.*** Let that be clearly understood on the record.) The Air Force came forward with a very simple proposition to the American public--forget about the Army, forget about the Navy, above all forget about the Navy. All you have to do is give us B-36s in large numbers; we have the atomic bomb and we'll take care of everything from now on. Nobody will ever need another soldier, never need another sailor. Omar Bradley said at the height of this, "There will never be another amphibious landing."**** This was about a week before Inchon.***** Almost. The American public bought it, largely. Fine, leave it all up to the boys in the wild blue yonder.

Q: A good public relations campaign, they had.

---

*Hoyt S. Vandenberg had been promoted to lieutenant general in March 1945.
**Senator W. Stuart Symington, first Secretary of the Air Force.
***The Latin quotation tells people to say nothing except good of the dead.
****General Omar N. Bradley, Chairman of the Joint Chiefs of Staff.
*****The U.S. amphibious landing at Inchon, Korea, in September 1950 dramatically reversed the fortunes of the Korean War.

Admiral Libby: Of course, we never could get anywhere with Vandenberg and Symington. We didn't get any help from the Army. They were fighting for their own; they were trying to keep the Air Force from taking everything the Army had. The Army had a lot of airplanes, and they wanted to keep them. The Army had the Redstone missile and wanted to keep that, and the Air Force was trying to take everything, get everything away from the armed services. They wanted to become the armed services of America, period. And they damned near got away with it.

Q: And a lot of Navy people suffered from it.

Admiral Libby: Of course they did. Along about this time things went from bad to worse, of course. Poor old Jim Forrestal had his breakdown and jumped out the window at Bethesda, and our altogether blessed Louie Johnson came in and took office as Secretary of Defense.* Louis Johnson and Harry Truman between them decided they would eradicate the Marine Corps instantly, first. The Army wanted to be rid of the Marine Corps, and Harry Truman had been in the Army so let's get rid of the Marine Corps. That was rule one. Rule two--- let's reduce the Navy to a service force. Give them some transports and some oilers and a few odds and ends, but the Air Force will take

---
*James V. Forrestal, Secretary of the Navy from 1944-1947 and first Secretary of Defense 1947-1949. Forrestal committed suicide shortly after leaving office. He jumped from a window at the Bethesda naval hospital, where he was being treated for mental strain and exhaustion.

care of everything, and the Army will take care of what the Air Force can't. That was Louis Johnson's motto as he started his famous program of "cutting the fat but not the muscle." The devastation was pretty widespread. I'll give you one example. They got some guy by the name of Meiling who came in to be the number one doctor in the Department of Defense.* Meiling promptly proceeded to close up every military hospital in the United States that he could get his hands on. He closed up half a dozen Navy hospitals, Long Beach, and all over the place, and wanted to turn everything over to the American Medical Association, private practice. Joel Boone turned in his suit at this point. Joel Boone was Surgeon General of the Navy and he had the guts to get up and tell Meiling he was all wet, and resigned; he quit; he just would have no part of it.** Somebody should ask Joel about this. This thing went from bad to worse, and finally we were meeting 18 hours a day, seven days a week, and I'm not exaggerating, in the Pentagon listening to Louie Johnson's hatchet man, General McNarney and going through the B-36 controversy.*** At this particular point

---

*Dr. Richard L. Meiling, Defense Department Director of Medical Services.
**Rear Admiral Joel T. Boone, Medical Corps, USN, was serving as chief of the Joint Plans and Action Division, Office of Medical Services, in the Office of the Secretary of Defense in early 1950. He criticized the plan to close some Army, Navy, and Air Force hospitals and to curtail services at others. As a result, he was reassigned in February 1950 as general inspector of naval medical activities for the Bureau of Medicine and Surgery. He retired from active duty later the same year.
***General Joseph T. McNarney, U.S. Air Force, Secretary Johnson's major advisor on fiscal and organizational matters. The Air Force sought to build a fleet of B-36s to enhance its strategic bombing capability.

the budget was allocated, backed up by Mr. Louie Johnson. As I recall it, the Air Force got something like 12 billion, the Army about eight billion, and the Navy got 2.6 billion. General McNarney then personally took $600 million away from the Navy's 2.6 billion and gave it to the Air Force to build B-36s with.

Everything was cut back, cut back, cut back. And at one budget meeting I remember, we were sitting there and General McNarney got up and said, "Now, the Navy isn't cooperating. The Navy has got to postpone the overhaul of these ships until next fiscal year so that it won't come out of this year's budget. We've got to show a saving. Put off the overhaul for another six months."

Then came Korea. The only thing that saved the Navy and the Marine Corps was Korea. If we hadn't had Korea, the Navy and the Marine Corps would have ceased to exist. That's a fact. The first thing that happened when Korea broke, they loaded up one of our transports. They put several Marine generals on it and started them out for Korea in a big way. It got two days out of port and broke down. Naturally. It hadn't had any overhaul.

So then everything turned and reversed itself. We used to have meetings every day. What can we do? What can we get going? The only shining light of the whole thing is that the day after Korea, Louie Johnson packed his bag and hammock and got out of town. We never heard of him again, but boy, he was as big a disaster in his own way as McNamara was in his.*

---

*Robert S. McNamara, U.S. Secretary of Defense, 1961-1968.

Libby #3 - 166

Q: For a shorter time.

Admiral Libby: The effects were nowhere as far-reaching.

Q: He wasn't there as long.

Admiral Libby: No, and he didn't have the billions of dollars to work with that McNamara had. He didn't have anything like the power that McNamara had. He was a short-timer. We got over him, but we'll never get over McNamara. We got over Louie Johnson, because the damage that he did was ephemeral. But we'll never recover from McNamara.

It was a very unfortunate period. A very unpleasant period. All of us were discouraged and tired and miserable and unhappy, and not getting anywhere, and frustrated simply because of this attitude which was prevalent that the Air Force could take care of everything.

Q: I was in Washington at the time, and I know what a terrible period it was for the Navy. When did Louie Denfeld turn in ...

Admiral Libby: Denfeld was fired on Navy Day, 1949, I think. I know it was Navy Day.*

Q: I know at this period that many naval officers had their opinions

---

*The announcement of Admiral Denfeld's firing was made on Navy Day, 27 October. He was actually detached from his duties as Chief of Naval Operations on 1 November 1949.

solicited as to this situation with the Air Force and in giving them received the ax because they were honest. I remember Admiral Bogan was one.*

Admiral Libby: Admiral Denfeld came back in late 1947 and was CNO for almost two years.

Q: It did terrible damage to lots of people's morale in the Navy.

Admiral Libby: Yes. My recollection is one of anger and frustration more than anything else. I remember when John L. Sullivan resigned he got a royal sendoff from the steps of the Pentagon.** He resigned when Louis Johnson cancelled the <u>United States</u> right after the keel had been laid, the new aircraft carrier. He turned in his suit then and there. A lot of us, at that time, felt that Admiral Denfeld would have been well advised to ask for retirement, too. Had he done so, we felt that public opinion would have reacted very unfavorably to the simultaneous resignation of the Secretary of the Navy and the stepping down of the Chief of Naval Operations over this rather arbitrary step.

Q: It would have been much more effective than to wait until he was fired.

---

*Vice Admiral Gerald Bogan, USN, relieved in July 1948 during the unification dispute.
**John L. Sullivan, Secretary of the Navy from September 1947 to May 1949.

Admiral Libby: Some of us suggested the idea to Admiral Denfeld, but he didn't go along with it, which I think was too bad. He would have been better off had he done so.

Q: Did he say why he didn't?

Admiral Libby: No. He just didn't.

Q: Who worked with you in that group?

Admiral Libby: A whole flock of people. It's hard to remember them all now. The usual OP-60, OP-06, OP-03 crowd, Freddie Boone, Matt Gardner, Arleigh Burke and a lot of others.* Rip Struble was OP-03; he was a Deputy for Plans and Policy.** He was Admiral Denfeld's operational deputy. He belonged to the junior chiefs of staff--the so-called OpDeps. He represented the Navy in the OpDeps meetings, and he was a primary spokesman in the Joint Chiefs of Staff meetings. Admiral Denfeld never had much to say when he was down at Joint Chiefs of Staff meetings. That was, I think, his Achilles' heel, really. He was very much interested in being Chief of Naval Operations, but he didn't enjoy being a member of the Joint Chiefs of Staff. That was his great weakness.

---

*Rear Admiral Walter F. Boone, USN; Rear Admiral Matthias B. Gardner, USN; Rear Admiral Arleigh Burke, USN.
**Vice Admiral Arthur D. Struble, USN.

Q: Was he not able to speak out and be forthright in expressing his opinion?

Admiral Libby: He left it all up to Rip Struble. That was really one of the unfortunate things about it, at the time.

Q: My records show, Admiral, that you also had additional duty as a member of the Permanent Joint Board of Defense, U.S.-Canada, during the time you were with CNO.

Admiral Libby: That is correct.

Q: I'd like to hear some information about that.

Admiral Libby: That was sort of additional duty. It was anything but full time. So that we not offend our cousins to the north of the border, who now couldn't care less apparently, under Mr. Pierre Trudeau, it's PJBD Canada-United States; not United States-Canada.[*] The Permanent Joint Board on Defense was an outgrowth of something called the Ogdensburg agreement between FDR and Prime Minister Mackenzie King of Canada, that predated World War II by four or five years, perhaps. It was then agreed (the meeting took place in Ogdensburg, New York) that Canada and the United States would cooperate in matters of mutual concern about the joint defense of the

---
[*]Pierre E. Trudeau, Prime Minister of Canada at the time of the interview.

Libby #3 - 170

North American continent. It was never reduced to a formal statement as to how to go about this, but the groundwork was laid then and there for this cooperation in defense matters between Canada and the United States. Of course, postwar the PJBD was quite active, and as far as I know it's still going on. I don't believe it's ever been abrogated.

Q: Where do they meet?

Admiral Libby: We used to meet once a quarter alternately in Canada and the United States and always at a military installation of some sort. The membership was identical on each side. We had a civilian chairman--in the case of the United States it was a retired Army general, Guy V. Henry, and in the case of Canada it was General, the Honorable A.G.L. McNaughton, but as they were retired, they were technically civilians.* Then we had an Army, a Navy, and an Air Force member and a State Department member on the United States side. They had an RCAF, a Royal Canadian Navy and a Canadian Army, and a Department of External Affairs member on the Canadian side. We had a small staff. We always had an agenda; we always dealt with matters of mutual concern, mutual interest, and the meetings usually lasted only two or three days. It was an intensely interesting assignment in a great many ways. We would meet alternately in the U.S. and Canada--in Halifax, in Toronto, in Edmonton, Alberta, and various odd places in

---

*Andrew G.L. McNaughton, Minister of National Defense, Canada, 1944-1945; Chairman, PJBD, 1945. Major General Guy V. Henry, U.S. Army (Retired).

Canada and the United States. We met at Annapolis, West Point, Key West, and a couple of Army posts. We always met once a quarter at some military installation, either in Canada or the United States, and we were sensible enough to pick the winter meetings in the United States and the summer meetings in Canada. It just so happened that that's the way it worked out. Except occasionally, we didn't. We got fouled up and went up to Argentia one time, or some such place, in the middle of winter. The meetings were always very fruitful. We had no executive powers. We made resolutions, and they would either be approved or not approved by our respective governments. I think we accomplished a lot.

Q: To whom would you make your reports--JCS?

Admiral Libby: No, they came out in the form of resolutions, and they went over to the White House, to the President and the Prime Minister, via the National Security Council.

General, the Honorable A.G.L. McNaughton was one of the most remarkable gentlemen that I've ever known in my life. He had the Canadian Army Contingent and went over to Europe in World War II. He had a row with Churchill and he came back home; he objected to the Canadians being decimated at Dieppe.* Anyway he and Churchill had a falling-out, so he came back to Canada. He was a very prominent

---

*Dieppe was the site of a disastrous Allied amphibious assault on German positions in France on 19 August 1942. Many of the raiders who were killed or captured were Canadians.

Canadian Army general, a long-time citizen of Canada. He knew more about Canada than all the rest of the Canadians put together. There wasn't any place in Canada he hadn't been. He was head of their Atomic Energy Commission; he was their delegate to the United Nations at one point. As far as I was concerned, he was Mr. Canada--he really knew more about Canada than anybody else combined, I think. He was an ardent sportsman, wonderful fisherman. We came back from White Horse to Edmonton one time, driving down the Alcan Highway, stopped off at Watson Lake about midnight (it was broad daylight) and A.G.L. decided he would go fishing. He borrowed some gear and promptly fell in. We ribbed him unmercifully about that.

The only times the meetings ever got sticky--we had some difficulty with our Canadian cousins right after Newfoundland and Labrador ceased to be British colonies and became incorporated into the Dominion of Canada. They were not part of the Dominion of Canada until quite recently, actually. We had made our leased base agreement with England, of course, about Newfoundland and Labrador, and not with Canada. After the war was over, England turned these two over to Canada, and they became provinces of Canada along with all the rest of them, so Canada wanted to make some changes in the leased base agreements to make sure they were in accordance with Canadian rather than with English laws. There were certain adjustments that had to be made and certain things that they wanted done that we were a little reluctant to do, so the negotiations got a little bit tight there for a while, but nothing ever really serious, nothing nasty--a little tense from time to time. That was the only time we had any trouble.

Q: Do you remember any other matters that came before the board?

Admiral Libby: They were routine matters—the matter of the troop stationing in Canada, the matter of the mutual Joint Air Defense, and all that kind of stuff.

Q: I think the one about Newfoundland and Labrador is an outstanding matter.

Admiral Libby: That was really sort of a problem that we had to wrestle with, and it took two or three meetings to get that ironed out.

Q: It's probable that without this board it would have come to a serious situation. The board was able to handle it.

Admiral Libby: No, I don't think that would have happened, but the board facilitated settling it much better. You know the way these negotiations can go on forever.

I have one anecdote about this business that always amused me. I don't think it would amuse the gentleman who is part of the story who has now risen to ambassadorship and high rank in the State Department, but at this time he was our State Department member, and I was the

Libby #3 - 174

Navy member. Something came up about this business, and we were talking about this transition of status for Labrador. We were meeting in a hotel in Montreal, I remember lots of red plush and high ceilings, and it was wintertime and colder than hell. Anyway, there was some document that we were trying to work up, and the State Department bloke and I were told to go into an anteroom and collaborate on the draft. We started in, and we sat there, and we wrote, and we wrote, and finally I said, "Bill, you and I are never going to get anywhere collaborating on this draft. We're just not going to be able to do it."

He said, "Why not?"

I said, "It's very simple. I was brought up by Admiral King, who taught me that if anything I wrote could be misunderstood, to go back and write it over again. You are a pupil of the State Department who taught you that if anything you write *can* be understood, go back and do it over again. You write your draft and I'll write mine." He blew his top, and we agreed that was what we would do, so he wrote his draft and I wrote mine, and we took it back and the board took their choice.

Q: Which one did they take? I would imagine that they took yours.

Admiral Libby: They did.

Q: Who is Bill?

Admiral Libby: I won't say. He rose to great heights in the State Department.

Q: Is he still in the State Department?

Admiral Libby: Yes, indeed. Very much so. He's an ambassador somewhere and a very good friend of mine, but we'd have been there yet if we had tried to collaborate on this draft.

Q: You were working from opposing viewpoints.

Admiral Libby: I wanted it to say something and he wanted it to say nothing.

Another amusing episode with Major General Bolte---Charlie was a chemical engineer by education; he came into the Army in World War I and liked it and stayed in; he got to be Deputy Chief of Staff of the Army, couldn't stand the Pentagon and turned in his suit after a year in the Pentagon.* He just couldn't take it. Charlie and I were up at West Point at the Thayer Hotel at one meeting. We got up there about late afternoon and we had an hour to kill before dinner. In our rooms at the Thayer Hotel was a little black book, which is equivalent to the Naval Academy _Reef_ _Points_, for the new cadet, to tell him the nuts and bolts about the Military Academy and helpful hints for expectant cadets. In it was the aptitude test that a candidate had to pass

---
*Major General Charles Bolte, U.S. Army.

before he could take the entrance exam to West Point. Charlie was then a major general in the Army, and I was a rear admiral in the Navy and we sat down at his desk and gave each other this aptitude test, and both of us busted cold—we couldn't pass it. We couldn't have qualified to take the entrance exams for West Point.

Charlie also had a firm conviction which he stated, that there was no disease on earth that an alcohol rub couldn't cure. His definition of an alcohol rub was to get a bottle of bourbon, drink the bourbon and rub yourself with an empty bottle. He's a great guy. He's still living around Washington, Alexandria.

By and large the PJBD is a very fine institution. I hope it's still flourishing, because it does a lot of good.

Q: You speak of being a rear admiral at this time, but we didn't pinpoint when this occurred.

Admiral Libby: I was selected when I was still on Admiral Denfeld's staff, and I made my number when I was coming back on the transport, in February of '48, I guess. So I came back to Washington as a very fresh-caught rear admiral.

Q: That was nice, wasn't it?

Admiral Libby: Yes. Much better than being a captain.

Libby #3 - 177

Q: Can we talk about your taking command of Cruiser Division Three? My date is September 1950.

Admiral Libby: It was after the Korean War had started, I know. The Korean War was going on, and I managed to get sprung from the Pentagon and rushed out to the Helena to take command. Chick Hartman had already left the ship; it was then in the navy yard getting overhauled.* He vacated the job, and I took it a couple of weeks later. When I left the Pentagon to go out and fight the Korean War, everybody said, "Coward." Why not? What a relief to get out of that goddamn place. I was never so happy in my life.

Anyway, we got the ship overhauled and got her re-ammunitioned, and whatnot, and joined up with the Toledo and started across. We got up to Yokuska. "Beauty" Martin had the fleet and "Hoke" Smith was out there in some capacity.** One of our earliest assignments was to go up to Wonsan Harbor and bombard Wonsan, briefly. We used to join up with the carrier task force and roam around the Sea of Japan. We shook down into a pretty fixed routine. We'd have a month on the line, a month on the Sea of Japan, two weeks to get back to Yokuska-- voyage repairs, battle damage, rest and recreation---and get back again. So it worked out four weeks on the line in the Sea of Japan conducting carrier operations, carrier strikes, gunfire support by the

---
*Rear Admiral Charles C. Hartman, USN.
**Vice Admiral Harold M. Martin, USN, Commander Seventh Fleet; Rear Admiral Allan E. Smith, USN, Commander Task Force 95 (Blockading and Escort Force).

cruisers, and so on, and then about four days back--eight days going and coming, and the rest of the time in Sasebo for about a week at a time.

Q: What were the carriers in your task force?

Admiral Libby: They changed. They were the regular standard aircraft carriers. I believe one was the *Princeton* at one point. We used to break loose and go off and shoot up the beach periodically whenever we would get a gunfire mission. We used to rush into Wonsan to defend the defenders of Wonsan periodically when the Koreans opened up. The Koreans had guns all over the place there in Wonsan Harbor, and we had a whole flock of ships in there from time to time just sort of to hold the place and keep it open and keep it out of the clutches of the North Koreans. Every now and then they would open up with shore batteries and we'd go into something called a war dance. We'd steam around at a high rate of steam and blaze back at them. These guns were field pieces really. They were on wheels; they would fire them and roll them back into a cave and then haul them out and fire them. I never understood why when the harbor was enveloped in a blinding fog, they never did open up. They could have raised hell with us if they had just opened up in the fog. You couldn't have seen where they were at all. They could have peppered the harbor; they might not have hit anything, but they would have made it very uncomfortable. But they never did that.

Libby #3 - 179

I remember one time the <u>Helena</u> hit one of those field pieces absolutely square on. You could see wheels and parts flying in the air--we really clobbered it. All the time we were in there, in and out, my flagship only got hit twice, and each time, if I'd had my choice where they hit us, they couldn't have done us less damage. They put one shell through the quarterdeck, aft; it went down into a living compartment and exploded in a mattress. There were feathers all over the compartment, but that's all the damage they did except for a hole in the deck. Another time they hit on the waterway under a 40-millimeter gun on the bridge and I saw this shrapnel fan out in the water. The only people who got wounded there were two kids who were running forward, and some of this shrapnel bounced off the inboard side of the lifeboat and nicked two of them through their life jackets. Both of them had life jackets on. They were just bruised; they weren't really hurt. We gave them Purple Hearts for their heroism. Some of the ships weren't so lucky, but we never got hurt.

As far as we were concerned, that war was drudgery like a lot of it is, you know. Just shooting, blazing away with the guns day and night and charging around with the carriers. The carrier boys worked their tails off. We used to go out from Yokuska about every six weeks, and whenever we took off you would see these kids on the carriers skylarking around and raising hell the way they did. Of course, in the summertime it was daylight almost all night long, so they had 22-hour day operations on those carriers. By the time they got ready to go back, those kids were just dropping in their tracks, the flight deck crews. They'd load the planes to take off and then just collapse. They were just completely worn out. They really had a rough time of it. But we on the cruisers and destroyers, it was monotony and boredom, a lot of gunfire and stuff but no running battle and no spectaculars---no submarines. Nobody ever found a submarine. But we got one destroyer mined one time.

Q: You were there for a year and a half.

Admiral Libby: Come November of that year I sent my cruiser division home, and I went up to Panmunjom. We actually didn't go out to the Western Pacific until about March '51 with the two cruisers and then in November '51 I sent the cruisers back and I went to Panmunjom.

Libby #4 - 181

Interview Number 4 with Vice Admiral Ruthven E. Libby, U.S. Navy (Retired)

Place: Admiral Libby's home, Coronado, California

Date: 7 June 1970

Subject: Biography

Interviewer: Commander Etta-Belle Kitchen, U.S. Navy (Retired)

Q: We're going to begin with your participation under ComNavFE as a United Nations delegate to the Korean truce talks, so I would like to have you start from the beginning and tell me all about your trip and who was there, what you did, and your reactions to these truce talks.*

Admiral Libby: That's rather a tall order, but we'll do the best we can. The beginning, I think, was when Admiral Turner Joy, instead of sending for me, which he normally would have done, he being ComNavFE also was senior United Nations delegate to the truce talk, came down to Yokuska and came aboard my flagship, the _Helena_, and asked me if I could be willing to go over to Panmunjom and relieve Arleigh Burke on the truce talks.** Arleigh wanted to be relieved, because he figured they weren't getting anywhere. I said, of course, I would, having known Admiral Joy for a long time and having a great deal of respect and admiration for him. So, as soon as the cruisers came home, I proceeded over to Panmunjom from Tokyo and he sent his private

---
*ComNavFE—Commander U.S. Naval Forces Far East.
**Vice Admiral C. Turner Joy, USN: Rear Admiral Arleigh Burke, USN.

airplane over for me, and I flew down to K-16 and then from K-16 by helicopter up to the apple orchard which is at a place called Munsan-ni.* It was known colloquially as the apple orchard, because that was what it had been, but it was a little Army encampment really and was the headquarters of the UN delegation. Admiral Joy lived there, and all the rest of us lived there, all the delegates, the staff.

Q: In Korea.

Admiral Libby: In Munsan-ni in South Korea just below the Inchon River. It's about half an hour by helicopter from Panmunjom, where the meetings took place. Panmunjom was a little place out in the prairie--a collection of tents with a sentry box on either side. There were main tents where we used to meet for plenary sessions and a couple of other tents where sub-delegations met, a press tent which was for our United States press section, and the Commies had comparable tents of their own scattered around about.

Q: Admiral Libby is showing me a picture of the layout at Panmunjom.

Admiral Libby: This photograph is one of several taken by an Army sergeant named Demetrio Borio. I never was too sure of his

---

*Airstrips in Korea were designated with a letter K combined with numbers.

credentials, but he was obviously a Russian. He seemed to be perfectly all right, and he certainly was a whiz of a photographer. Whatever happened to him, I don't know, but he took a whole series of photographs all through this. This one in particular is a very good example of the layout at Panmunjom. Panmunjom was in the so-called demilitarized zone, so-called Holy Land by the Marine aviators, because every time the Commies wanted to make a fuss about something they would accuse us of having violated the DMZ, the same thing that's going on in Vietnam today.

The two white tents (in the photograph), one in the foreground behind the two white sentry boxes is the main conference tent where all the plenary sessions were held whenever we had the full delegation meeting. The two off to the right of that are tents where the sub-delegations used to meet. My own was the prisoner of war delegation, and we had two or three others. The olive drab one immediately to the right of the big conference tent was our press tent, where we used to meet with all the press representatives, and there were thousands of them. On the right of that is our own U.S. tent, where we used to meet preliminarily to the plenary sessions of the meeting with the Communist sub-delegations. The Communist headquarters is the lone tent well off to the left. The two sentry boxes which you see, one of them ours, the other one was the Communists'. The two sentries used to stand outside these sentry boxes and glare at each other and glare at us as we went through. We didn't pay too much attention to them. The locale was primarily a farm with a couple of thatched huts in the foreground. The area originally had been used to grow ginseng root, which is supposed to be a very potent drug the Koreans think will cure any ailment known to man or beast. All in all this was a formidable spot, particularly in wintertime when everything was covered with snow and ice. Once you got off the helicopter pad, it was mud and you floundered around. The one thing that used to burn the Communists up completely was that we had helicopters and they didn't. They felt a great loss of face. We had only a good old HUP, one of the earlier helicopters, and when the weather was at all passable and the thing didn't break down, we would always go to and from by chopper.*

Q: How far were you from the place you stayed?

Admiral Libby: About half an hour as the helicopter flew, about two hours over almost impassable roads by jeep if the helicopter couldn't fly. There had been a bridge right across the river there but the bridge was demolished and to get up to Panmunjom by road, we had to go pretty well inland and it was quite a haul, probably 60 miles but it was a hard, long, grueling trip over almost non-existent roads.

Q: How far did the Communists have to travel?

---

*The HUP was a Piasecki-built helicopter known as the "flying banana" because of its shape.

Admiral Libby: They came down, I think, from Kaesong, which wasn't very far away, and much better roads from Kaesong and Panmunjom than there were from Panmunjom and the apple orchard.

The Communists had two very distinct delegations: the Chinese People's Volunteers headed by Hsieh Fang, obviously the brains of the whole outfit; and the North Korean delegation headed by Nam Il.[*] A Korean Army General Lee Sang Cho was opposite me in the prisoner of war delegations.[**] I never dealt with any delegations except the POW delegation and good old Lee Sang Cho. The procedures were pretty well stereotyped in the plenary sessions, and it became perfectly obvious early on in the game that the brains of the organization were the Chinese. Hsieh Fang was a very ordinary looking guy and, of course, the Chinese went in for utterly nondescript uniforms, padded cotton in the winter and sort of a military looking cotton with a military jacket with a high collar in the summertime but no insignia of rank of any kind. It was perfectly obvious that the Chinese were really in charge, although presumably the head of the delegation was the North Korean general, Nam Il. He was always immaculately turned out with leather boots and a snappy blue uniform, all this insignia of rank, and whatnot, and a cigarette holder, long cigarettes. He looked like an Adolph Menjou of the military.[***] He was a pretty smart cookie, himself, but obviously he was subservient to Hsieh Fang.

The procedure, of course, was that whichever side wanted to open

---

[*]Major General Hsieh Fang, Chinese Communist forces.
[**]Major General Lee Sang Cho, North Korean People's Army.
[***]Adolph Menjou was a dapper-looking movie actor of that era.

would say, "I will make a statement." Admiral Joy would start to make the statement, and it would be translated as he went along, first into Korean, then into Chinese. I'm perfectly convinced that Hsieh Fang spoke and understood English perfectly, but he never let on that he did. He had an interpreter who had been wounded in the bombing, I believe. He had gone to school in Oxford, he was an Oxford graduate. The interpreter was obviously an embittered little guy. He hated everybody, and he hated us. He was obviously a rabid convert to Communism. The Korean interpreter was a little fellow who had been a professor at the university in Seoul and his family had been captured, I believe, and dragged back to North Korea when the first invasion took place; I think that little guy was more or less a hostage. He acted as an interpreter for the North Koreans, but he always looked very unhappy, and I don't think his heart was in his work at all. He was an interpreter between English and Korean and this other guy was interpreter between English and Chinese. Of course, we had interpreters on our side. We had the Underwood brothers who were sons of missionaries and had been born in Korea and spent all their lives there.* They were our Korean interpreters and we had a Chinese captain, as smart as a whip, who was our Chinese interpreter. We'd check back and forth--he knew what the Chinese said. It was a slow and laborious process getting everything said back and forth so that you could understand, because it had to be translated in three ways.

---

*Lieutenant Horace G. Underwood, USN, and First Lieutenant Richard F. Underwood, AUS.

A simple statement that could be read in ten minutes took at least an hour to get through, back and forth.

If you haven't read Admiral Joy's book, How Communists Negotiate, that should be read, and it should be written right into this tape because it explains the whole pitch much better than I could.*

Q: I want to get your reactions to it.

Admiral Libby: My reactions were just that. As I say, it was perfectly obvious that the Communist approach was to make a flat statement and stick with it, knowing perfectly well there wasn't a shred of truth in what they said. There's no negotiating with them, there's no arguing with them, there's no dealing with them as you and I would deal if we wanted to dicker over selling an automobile or arranging anything. Any logical negotiation just doesn't exist in their book; they just don't understand the meaning of the word.

Bob Lovett, when he was Deputy Secretary of Defense, said very aptly, "Ordinary negotiation is a matter of quid pro quo--with the Communists it's a matter of quid pro quid."** They just take a position and the position is one they know perfectly well you can't

---

*Admiral C. Turner Joy, USN(Ret.), How Communists Negotiate (New York: The Macmillan Company, 1955). Another informative book on the subject is William H. Vatcher, Jr., Panmunjom: The Story of the Korean Military Armistice Negotiations (New York: Frederick A. Praeger, Inc., 1958).
**Robert A. Lovett, Deputy Secretary of Defense, 1950-1951, Secretary of Defense, 1951-1953.

possibly buy, and they never budge from that position. They just drag the negotiations on and on and resort to invective and lies and trumped-up events and everything else hoping that eventually, through sheer exasperation, you'll say, "To hell with it--let's get on to something else." And they will have won that point. That's pretty much what happened out there in Korea.

I was with them for seven months, and the negotiations dragged on and on. It finally took me about a good three months, or a bad three months, depending on how you look at it, beating these people over the head, before we could even exchange lists of prisoners of war, which they had and which we had. Finally, when they agreed to exchange lists of POWs, they gave us a list of something like 1,300 or 2,000 POWs, about one-tenth of what we knew they had taken, and we gave them a list of something like 15,000 or 16,000. They came into the POW negotiation with Lee Sang Cho's first approach of, "We will simply agree today to exchange prisoners of war and let everybody go home." That was his proposal and he wouldn't vary from that for three months. It took me three months to get him to exchange lists of POWs. That gives you a rough idea. Meanwhile, all sorts of invective.

We met almost every day. There were a few times when we didn't meet. Occasionally there would be a recess called, and it was very noticeable--you could always tell how badly shook they were by the length of the recess. If there was some fairly simply problem which could be settled by reference to Peiping, it didn't take very long. But if it had to go all the way back to Moscow, it took maybe a week or two-week recess while they sent it back to the boss man to decide what could be done about it. There wasn't any question that Russia was very much involved in this thing and that insofar as I say, as a controlling voice among the delegations, it was the Chinese who were running the show. Nam Il was a pretty shrewd guy, but he was stupid compared to Hsieh Fang; he was really a very unusual individual. I don't know what ever happened to him, but it's too bad he was a Communist, because he was a smart cookie.

Q: Did you ever know where he was educated?

Admiral Libby: I don't know. I know nothing about him, but he was really quite a boy.

I headed the U.S. side of the prisoner of war delegation, and we had all this mess about voluntary repatriation. We got orders from Washington to plunk for voluntary repatriation. In other words, we didn't have to send any Commie POW back that didn't want to go. This voluntary repatriation business was something which completely horrified all of us in the military. It was something that had never been heard of before. Prisoners of war were prisoners of war, and when you exchange prisoners of war, you send the enemy back his and you get yours. But it came in from Washington and apparently somebody in Washington, presumably in the State Department, thought it would be a wonderful idea--it would make very fine propaganda, and all that sort of baloney. Then, of course, what it did was create unending complications, and it created an awful lot of bad blood, not that that was too important. In my own mind, it raised a very interesting point and that point is simply this: If one of the Communist prisoners that we had captured refused to be repatriated and elected to go on our side, he was a hero. Of course, the handful of people on our side who chose to go with the Communists were bums. That didn't make any sense to any of us that that should ever be part of it in the first place. We had a handful of people who had been brainwashed and who were general misfits; they would probably be the protestors of today. There weren't more than 25 or 30 altogether who elected to stay with the Communists. They've all come back since with their tail between their legs, but, of course, they were all given bad conduct discharges from our service and generally regarded by our people as bums, because they chose to do what the other side did and became to us heroes. It didn't make any sense to us.

But we were stuck with it, and we had to try to sell it to the Commies, and it outraged them and they let us know that they wanted no part of it. That was one of the sticking blocks of ever getting the armistice arranged. It probably caused as much trouble as anything.

Q: Did they know that you didn't like it either?

Admiral Libby: No, we never let on that we didn't like it. We couldn't. But they didn't like it, because they wanted their people back--they wanted all of them. They probably wanted to kill most of them for ever having committed the crime of having gotten captured. In a sense, you can't blame a lot of them for not wanting to go back. Actually, it was hard to tell exactly how voluntary the Chinese volunteers were. They don't have much to say about what they do. They probably were conscripted and dragged into serving in the armed forces in the first place, and a lot of them probably weren't very keen on Communism in the second place. The idea may have been a good humanitarian gesture on our part and also wonderful propaganda against Communism, which we were trying to discredit, of course. A lot of people elected not to go back, but it certainly put us on the horns of a dilemma even with our own people, and it created, I think, a very bad military precedent.

Anyway, this voluntary repatriation business held up the arrival of the achievement of an armistice for some months, I'm quite sure.

There were other features about the negotiations which we found a little disturbing. There was a basic impatience, it seemed to us, back in Washington, because we weren't getting any farther than we were. I know at one point the State Department sent out Mr. U. Alexis Johnson, who has since risen high in the echelons of the State Department, to come out to the apple orchard and see what was going on. His general approach was that we didn't know what we were up to, we didn't know how to negotiate, and if we were sensible people we'd have gotten much forwarder than we had by now. That's the way he apparently felt at the time. I don't say he feels that way now or that he actually did feel that way, but that's the impression we got.

I don't know whether we converted him otherwise. On a great many occasions we would get absolutely ridiculous orders from the Joint Chiefs of Staff, through Tokyo (whoever was in charge, General MacArthur, General Ridgway, and finally Mark Clark.* We didn't have any trouble with Mark Clark but we did with Ridgway, particularly) to do something which we on the spot knew would have been next door to fatal--not only stupid, but it would have pulled the rug completely out from under us. Every time that we were able to get the general in Tokyo to go back to Washington and request that the orders be changed they were. There was never any question about it; if we protested, they always said okay but on some occasions we couldn't get Tokyo to go back to Washington, so we were stuck. Of course, that was quite understandable, because General Ridgway was a damn good soldier and he believed in obeying orders--if he got orders from Washington to do it, okay. I happened to know that as far as the Joint Chiefs of Staff were concerned there was an Air Force lieutenant colonel who was down on the tank (the Joint Staff) who was monitoring Panmunjom for the Joint Chiefs of Staff. He wrote out most of the stuff, and a lot of it was rubber-stamped by the Joint Chiefs and came out to us from the JCS. Some of them were idiotic things we were able to cancel, but some things we couldn't. We'd reach an impasse; we'd get our feet set in concrete, or things would come to a grinding halt and we would just

---

*The following individuals served as Commander in Chief United Nations Command and Commander in Chief U.S. Far East Command: General of the Army Douglas MacArthur, 1950-1951; General Matthew B. Ridgway, 1951-1952; General Mark W. Clark II, 1952-1953.

about get ready to persuade the Communists to give, and then we'd get flat orders from Washington to give in ourselves. So we lost out a little at a time over the months by direct order from Washington, and it was pretty discouraging.

Q: Do you have a for instance?

Admiral Libby: I don't remember any details but I mean little bits and pieces, various points on the agenda--it's all in Admiral Joy's book. He mentioned a couple of for instances of some importance. The point was that nobody in Washington understood what we were up against, because nobody had been up against this sort of thing before. Unfortunately, they haven't learned by our experience; that's the thing that bothers me.

Q: The two things are so similar that it's almost frightening, except that in the Korean War at least they did keep fighting, whereas in the Vietnamese they stopped at the time of the so-called truce talks.

Admiral Libby: That's right. The Paris talks were an absolute carbon copy of what went on in Panmunjom--the attitude of the Communists. They just get set, and you get nowhere. They just flatly won't negotiate. Anybody who ever bothered to read this little book of Admiral Joy's would know perfectly well that would happen. To me it's incomprehensible that nobody bothered to learn about what we went through.

Q: It's one of the early indications of not permitting people to do the job from the operational commander level which has been carried to such extremes at this present time.

Admiral Libby: It's been proved right down to the last comma and period about the way the Communists behave at the negotiating table. If they think that they have anything to gain by stalling, they will stall. We are never going to get anywhere in Paris. We might just as well bring everybody home, as long as they don't put the military heat on the North Vietnamese. The Commies will never budge unless they are being hurt militarily and being hurt badly. The worse they are being hurt, the more amenable they are to negotiating. It's just as simple as that.

Q: If I were a North Vietnamese, I'd feel the same way, too.

Admiral Libby: Certainly.

Q: You can't expect them to think we're the good guys and they're going to treat us nice just because ...

Admiral Libby: All they've got to do now is just hang on, and we'll throw in the towel eventually. They are convinced of that and they have every reason to think so.

Admiral Joy came home about mid-April of '52, and General Harrison, who had been his Army deputy, relieved him. I stayed until the end of June, and then I came home.* John Daniel relieved me, a rear admiral, had been in BuPers.** I don't know how long he was there. They eventually worked out a system whereby, and I think it's still in effect, the term out there is something like six months. Now they still have an Armistice Commission. There had never been a peace treaty. The Military Armistice Commission meets every now and again. They have a system now whereby the senior U.S. official is either a rear admiral or a brigadier general, or if it's an Air Force bloke, he's a brigadier general in the Air Force. It's generally a fairly junior, sometimes it may be an upper half, not normally a junior admiral, and the term is only six months, and then they get relieved. I think John Daniel may have been there from July until the armistice was finally signed.

The big recreation was pitching horseshoes. The experts at the horseshoe game were General Turner, the Air Force guy, and Buddy Ferenbaugh, the Army boy.*** Buddy Ferenbaugh had been in command of a tank regiment, and he was relieved from that and came down to take over as the Army deputy. General Turner, I think, had been with the Fifth Air Force. Both he and Buddy Ferenbaugh were huge individuals---

---

*Major General William K. Harrison, Jr., USA, who was promoted to lieutenant general during the course of his tenure as senior delegate.
**Rear Admiral John C. Daniel, USN.
***Major General Howard McM. Turner, USAF; Major General Claude B. Ferenbaugh, USA.

great big people. We always said it wasn't fair. They could just lean over and put the horseshoe on the peg; they didn't have to throw it. They were pretty much the champs. That's about all we did. The youngsters played volleyball, and we played horseshoes and went for walks around the countryside. There was nothing to do at all. It was very pleasant in the summer—hot and dry, long days—but in the winter it was pretty grim. I lived there through the winter.

One very interesting episode. I relieved Arleigh Burke and in the course of the relief process, he had an electric blanket which he sold me. When he got back to Washington I discovered he had made 50 cents on the deal. He had sold me a secondhand blanket for 50 cents more than he paid for it.

Q: Were you ever humiliated during the truce talks? In the early days, my recollection of history is that the North Koreans and Chinese attempted to humiliate their opposite numbers.

Admiral Libby: They tried, but they never made it. When the truce talks were first initiated at Kaesong, they tried very hard to humiliate the American delegation. Admiral Joy, Hank Hodes, and Arleigh Burke went up there to Kaesong and the Communists tried to make it appear that the Americans were suing for peace, that they (the Communists) were the victors and we were there with our tail between our legs—that we had been defeated and we wanted out.* That was the

---
*Major General Henry I. Hodes, USA.

impression they tried to put over. As Admiral Joy wrote in his book, he discovered when they first met at the conference table that they had sawed the legs off the chairs on the American side and built them up on the Communist side so the Communists sat up high looking down. Everything they had was of larger scale--taller flags.

What had happened was--my memory is hazy on this and I don't vouch for it completely--when a Russian, Malik, I believe, indicated in a public address that it might be a good idea if some truce talks were held.* Then General MacArthur or Ridgway first proposed that the meeting be held on a neutral ship in Wonsan Harbor, or some such place--a neutral ship in fairly well enemy controlled waters; but the Commies would have none of that. We made all kinds of efforts to hold the thing under an aura of true neutrality and, of course, got nowhere. Finally, it was agreed that they would hold them in Kaesong. Then it became very evident what the Commies were up to--that they were trying to make it look as though the Americans had been roundly defeated and were just suing for peace. Our delegates were being insulted and harassed and had machine guns poked at them and all that kind of stuff. I'm quite sure it was Ridgway who said, "Okay. No more. Finished. Quit this monkey business." Then they were finally set up at Panmunjom. It was only at Kaesong that it took place, this business of trying to humiliate us.

---

*On 23 June 1951, Yakov A. Malik, Soviet delegate to the United Nations, advocated a Korean cease-fire and armistice on the UN radio program "Price of Peace," on the Columbia Broadcasting System (CBS).

Q: What was the article in The New York Times concerning you?

Admiral Libby: Lee Sang Cho got out of line one day, and I told him he was getting too big for his britches, and that was widely reported. You'd be surprised how many people took issue with me for being too flippant. More people approved than disapproved but somebody always disapproves. I don't imagine that there's ever been more miles of celluloid exposed than there were at us. Every time we came out of the tent, a whole battery of people would want to know what went on, and we told them what we could. We couldn't tell them too much.

The poor press people must have led a dog's life. They had something called a press train parked in a siding outside one of the towns in the general vicinity of Panmunjom. It was almost inaccessible. They lived on this train, and if you can imagine living on a train, parked on a siding, and some of them were there for months. Rembert James, one of our people now with the Copley News Service was on that press train--lived there for months. We had a couple of Communists--one named Burchett who was from Australia, I believe. We had another one who was a Britisher who was an avowed out-and-out Communist. I always suspected one of the guys from The New York Times as being about as far left as he could get, but that I couldn't prove, but I know that the other two were Communists. They were slimy individuals, if I ever saw any. The Britisher and the Australian--somehow you sort of can understand a Korean or a Russian being that way, but it's a pretty grim thing to confront when you have some of what you consider to be your own people subverted the way they were. They were really vicious; they were bad.

Q: In their reporting of the news?

Admiral Libby: In the questions they asked and their general attitude, snotty behavior. They were just as Communist as the Koreans and the Chinese, and they acted accordingly. They were just bad people to deal with.

Q: Do you recall any episodes during the period in which you were in Korea that were not related in Admiral Joy's book?

Admiral Libby: I don't recall any of any importance. The Communists were periodically trying to stage incidents; they were trying to accuse us of all kinds of outrages, and they were trying to do all this, that, and the other. Colonel Murray and some of the others on the staff were always going off to investigate these alleged incidents--none of them ever turned out to have any validity, but we thought it ought to be proved that if anything happened at all the Communists had staged it deliberately to create a fuss.*

One of the Communists' stocks in trade in negotiating was to accuse you of all sorts of high crimes and misdemeanors to prove that you were not behaving in good faith. They were always alleging that

---
*Colonel James C. Murray, USMC, a United Nations Command liaison officer.

we violated the demilitarized zone, or trying to indicate that we had, or trying to prove that we were guilty of all sorts of odds and ends, so they would occasionally stage some incident. None that I know of that ever was investigated by the liaison people ever turned out to have any validity at all. It was obviously staged by the Communists. They never got away with it, but they never quit trying.

Q: Was your reaction one of, "Well, I guess this is the way the thing is," or were you frustrated, or did you get mad?

Admiral Libby: We learned early on, never lose your temper, because you'd be had if you did. It was very good tactics to appear to get furious with them, but you had to do it deliberately. I used to read them out regularly, but I did it deliberately. The only way you could get through to them was to insult them sometimes. It's pretty hard to insult a Communist, but if you insult him, he'll at least deviate from the routine of repeating the same old lies day after day after day.

Q: Can you remember any of those incidents?

Admiral Libby: I just mentioned one. Lee Sang Cho made some threat or some ultimatum that if we didn't do thus and so they would demolish us, and I simply told him he was getting too big for his britches. He was pretty stupid. He wasn't one of their leading lights by any manner of means. I tell you, this Hsieh Fang was really something.

He was very smooth; he never, apparently, lost his equanimity; never lost his temper, seldom raised his voice, but he was obviously a pretty strong character in that outfit. As I say, there was no question about the Chinese running the show. The North Koreans were just their window dressing. This was, of course, after the Chinese had come in.

Q: Who did you have on your staff besides yourself and your interpreter?

Admiral Libby: We had a sizable staff. Admiral Joy, General Harrison, General Ferenbaugh, General Turner, Hank Briggs (Admiral Joy's flag secretary), Colonel Murray, two or three Air Force colonels, the Underwood brothers who were Korean interpreters, Captain Lee, a little Chinese boy who was the Chinese interpreter, Bill Nuckols who was an Air Force public information officer.[*] He had a lieutenant colonel who was his assistant. Then we had the usual staff assistants--commanders, lieutenant commanders. One of the people I had in my POW delegation was Oswald Jacoby.[**] He was in the Navy during the war and one of my POW boys. He had quite a staff. The routine was, we used to get together--the main delegations, the plenary delegation, didn't meet every day but the sub-delegations, one

---

[*]Captain Henry M. Briggs, USN; Lieutenant Horace G. Underwood, USN, and First Lieutenant Richard F. Underwood, AUS; Brigadier General William P. Nuckols, USAF.
[**]Lieutenant Commander Oswald Jacoby, USNR, was also one of the foremost U.S. tournament bridge players.

or another of them, met almost every day. There would be a plenary session, main delegation, not every day but very frequently. Before we ever went up, we would have gotten together in the main tent. We would have prepared our position paper, knew what we were going to say about what, worked them all up, got them all cleared by the admiral so that everything was hunky-dory, so we knew exactly what we were going to say before we got up there. We frequently, of course, had to ad lib, but we knew basically what we were going to do, what we were going to say. We established the party lines, the policy of what we were going to follow. Then for the plenary session we did the same thing. Everybody contributed to the staff papers, and it was normal military staff work. When we came back we would brief the admiral as to what had gone on in our particular sub-delegation so he was cognizant of the whole thing and knew what was going on.

Q: How many were there in your sub-delegation?

Admiral Libby: Myself and my legal officer, and Oswald Jacoby. I generally had one of the Underwood brothers as my own interpreter, but it varied sometimes. There were a couple of youngsters who helped do the paperwork. I probably left out some very important people, because I can't remember specifically more than that.

Q: In your meetings, sub-meetings, there would be three of you and three of the North Koreans?

Admiral Libby: There would always be an opposite number. For everybody on my delegation the Communist side would have twice as many, because they had a Korean and a Chinese. Take for example a plenary session: there would be the admiral and there would be the Army, Navy, and Air Force people, and our interpreters, and some of the staff behind us, and on the other side there would be the same setup with the Koreans and the Chinese and in back of them would be 60 or 70 people--always. Any Communist delegation had twice as many principals as you had and they had a backup force of at least 60 Commies back of the main delegation busily writing out everything that was said. They had to have somebody watching everybody. Somebody had to watch everybody to make sure he didn't do the wrong thing. I don't know how they ever run a Communist state, I really don't. It must be the most ponderous thing in the world. I don't know how they possibly do it, because, as I say, everybody with the slightest bit of authority has to be watched by at least two other people. It must be a mess.

Q: I've often wondered how the Russians could possibly have an organization that would function when everybody works for somebody else.

Admiral Libby: I don't know. It doesn't function very well. It functions through sheer bureaucratic weight. It's almost like our Department of Defense under Mr. McNamara. That didn't function at all, but it certainly spent a lot of money.

Q: Did you feel that you accomplished anything in the seven months you were there?

Admiral Libby: I think so, yes. I learned a great deal personally. I only wish I could get the word around and that people would learn by what we learned out there, but they didn't and haven't. We laid the groundwork for what eventually became the armistice, if that's any accomplishment. I think we accomplished something. It cost Admiral Joy his life, of course. He was killed out there just as surely as if he had been shot. My tent was right across the walk from his tent. He had a big tent; I had a small one. He used to keep me awake all night with his coughing--not keep me awake all night, but you could hear him coughing his head off all night. We had a little Army doctor, a captain in the Army Medical Corps, who used to give him what he could, but it turned out when the admiral got back to the Naval Academy, after he had been relieved, that what he had was viral pneumonia and didn't realize it---nobody knew it. So it went on into anemia, and that went into pernicious anemia and he eventually died of leukemia; but it was a result of that siege out there.* He was a war casualty just as much as if he had gotten shot dead---no question about it.

---

*Admiral Joy served as Superintendent of the Naval Academy from August 1952 to August 1954, then died in June 1956 at the age of 61.

I think we accomplished something. We'd have accomplished a lot more if we had been let alone---if we hadn't been told to give here and give there. Under the circumstances we accomplished a certain amount, I think.

One rather amusing incident of which I was not a part, or a party---we had all the Chinese and North Korean POWs locked up on the island of Koje Do. There was a young brigadier general in the Army, Dodd, who managed to get himself captured by the POWs.[*] He wandered in the compound and they captured him. Here was the commanding general of the POW island captured by the POWs! Mark Clark was boiling over, and we held a session on what was to be done. We agreed that he would have to be expended; we wouldn't give in to the POW demands. Eventually, they turned him loose, after a day or two, and the Army promptly busted him from brigadier general to colonel. The first thing that this misguided individual did was to hold a press conference on Koje Do, where he informed all assembled that the Army couldn't do this to him. Some reporter said, "Colonel, you have just made lieutenant colonel. Would you like to try for major?"

Q: Were you glad when you were relieved?

Admiral Libby: I was very glad. It was a frustrating experience in a lot of ways, and it got a little boring, but it was truly educational,

---
[*] Brigadier General Francis T. Dodd, USA, commandant of the Koje Island stockade.

and I don't regret having been over there at all. All I wish is that every American could go through a couple of weeks of it and thus learn what they're up against. People just haven't any conception of the way Communists behave and operate. They're going to find out, of course, when this country gets taken over by them. These kids that are busily engaged in trying to bring the country down are not going to like what they bring down around their own ears if they succeed. There's no use telling them; they've got to find out for themselves.

Q: It's a frightening prospect.

Admiral Libby: It is. I don't know what you can do about it. It seems to me it gets a little worse every day; they get more out of line and more unreasonable.

Q: When you came back to Washington you were assigned as Assistant Chief of Naval Operations for Operations. The dates I have are August '52 until '54. During this period there were changes in the Navy again and as an Assistant Chief of Naval Operations you were close to the head of it. Can you describe some episodes during that time?

Admiral Libby: I believe that this was just a normal routine in Washington; things were rocking along pretty much as they always were--the battle of the budget which is a standard routine in Washington. As I recall, at this time the Secretary of Defense was

Charlie Wilson.* He initiated the first of what we used to call the Secretary of the Defense's clambakes down in Quantico. The top people in Washington went down and took over the FBI Academy and lived there and lived in the various Marine quarters for about a week. It was a very good idea of Charlie Wilson's to get everybody together and get them to know each other better. It was quite pleasant. We had business sessions in the forenoon and played golf or whatever, in the afternoon, and then there was always some sort of entertainment after dinner. It was a very pleasant, very worthwhile three or four days. I think Charlie Wilson originated this and various other Secretaries kept it up. The last one I went to, Neil McElroy was Secretary.** To everyone's consternation, we discovered at this particular clambake we not only had morning and afternoon sessions, but evening sessions, too, so they just transferred the Pentagon down to Quantico, where the results were not as salubrious as they had otherwise been.

I remember on the first clambake that Charlie Wilson held, I'm sure this is not in any official record--Wilfred J. McNeil was Assistant Secretary of Defense.*** (He was comptroller, a budget man for SecDef. As such, he controlled the purse strings pretty much.) In order to mix everybody up, he and Curt LeMay were assigned a room together at the FBI Academy.**** Curt LeMay was Deputy Chief of Staff of the Air Force at the time and he and McNeil had had a few official

---
*Charles E. Wilson, Secretary of Defense from 1953 to 1957.
**Neil H. McElroy, Secretary of Defense from 1957 to 1959.
***Wilfred J. McNeil, Comptroller of the Department of Defense.
****General Curtis E. LeMay, U.S. Air Force.

fireworks, but it worked out fine; everything was all right. That was a particular time when I first discovered what a unique character Curt LeMay is. That man could do anything. He was absolutely a completely natural-born athlete. He didn't play golf, but part of the festivities were a driving contest at the seventh hole on the course down there. The Secretary of the Navy had gone out and he had driven the ball 295 yards, or something like that, Charlie Thomas, and he had his flag parked out there.* Curt LeMay went out there one afternoon and borrowed a driver, a ball, and he smacked it down the fairway, and outdrove Charlie Thomas by about 40 yards. He won that contest hands down. He broke the all-time record at the FBI shooting academy--that business that they had with surprise shooting, and whatnot. With a pistol he went through there and smashed everything. That guy could do anything, practically amazing physical prowess. Of course, he was a ham radio operator of considerable fame. Quite a guy. I regret that he decided to run for vice president with Mr. Wallace.** That didn't do him any good.

As I recall it, there wasn't anything particularly un-routine during this period, nothing shattering happened.

Q: And then you went for almost two years to command the Battleship-Cruiser Force, U.S. Atlantic Fleet.

---

*Charles S. Thomas was Secretary of the Navy from May 1954 to April 1957.
**LeMay was the vice presidential candidate on George Wallace's third party ticket in 1968.

Admiral Libby: That's right. I was detached from Washington and went down to Norfolk and took command of BatCruLant. My flagship was the <u>Albany</u>. We had a very good setup on that. Jimmy Holloway originally had dreamed it up.* With a small cruiser as a flagship, there wasn't much room for full staff aboard ship. So he had set up his logistics staff ashore at Norfolk and just kept an operational staff aboard ship with him, and I carried on with the same business, and it worked out very well. All the nuts and bolts of running the show were done by the staff ashore, and my operational staff aboard ship with me: we had room enough to handle it. But there again that was primarily routine. There was nothing unusual about that.

Shortly after I relinquished the job and went back up to Washington, they decommissioned all the battleships so I was the last ComBatCruLant that had battleships. My relief had cruisers only. During that particular period, I took the midshipmen on two cruises to Europe, and I made one deployment to the Mediterranean, making like a CruDiv command. In other words we had myself and, I think, two cruiser division commanders, rear admirals, perhaps three, but we had to keep a CruDiv commander over in the Mediterranean with the Sixth Fleet and deployments got a little tight, so I took one tour over there, January through April, as a CruDiv commander, and let the other boys stay home for a change. I found out early on why, in the old days, the naval wars in the Mediterranean always took place in the summertime. Along about September they simply hauled their triremes

---

*Rear Admiral James L. Holloway, Jr., USN, served as ComBatCruLant from 1950 to 1953.

up on the beach, and they stayed out of the ocean until spring. We were over there from January through April, and in that whole period we had something like four days of good weather. The rest of the time it was just rougher than Billy-be-damned. The Med is about a foot deep, very shallow, and the wind springs up and that can get really rough. We had some very interesting experiences in that respect as far as rough weather was concerned, but there again, nothing out of the ordinary.

I was then riding the _Iowa_, and we had to go up to Istanbul. We finally got up there late one afternoon. It was about late February or early March, and it was snowing. It never snows in Istanbul, but it did that day. I went ashore to pay my official calls, and I had to go through the Byzantine stables and I had to go into a mosque and I got back from that and I was just absolutely frozen solid.

Then, as I say, we took the midshipmen on two successive cruises. The first year we got back to Norfolk around early August (the midshipmen cruises used to last June and July and August in my day; they have cut them back to only two months, June and July) and we spent the next two and a half months going to sea to duck hurricanes. We had one hurricane after another that particular fall. There wasn't anything very world-shaking about that tour either.

Q: Were you aware of the Russian buildup in the Mediterranean when you were over there?

Libby #4 - 211

Admiral Libby: No. It hadn't started yet. That's very new. This was in the middle Fifties. There wasn't a Russian within miles of the Mediterranean in those days. The Mediterranean belonged to us.

Q: The fact that the Geneva Conference had set the boundary line for North and South Vietnamese and our advisors being sent in wasn't felt by the Navy in those years either. The four years from '54, '56, '58--the last two years of that time you came back to Washington again as Deputy Chief of Naval Operations for Fleet Operations and Readiness.

Admiral Libby: I relieved Bobby Briscoe, but only very briefly.[*] Then Matt Gardner decided to retire. He was OP-06. When Admiral Carney became Chief of Naval Operations, he split OP-03, which used to be Plans and Policy, Fleet Operation and Readiness.[**] He split that into two, OP-03, which became Fleet Operations and Readiness, and OP-06 became Plans and Policy, and Matt Gardner was the head of OP-06.[***] I got through being ComBatCruLant and I came up and I had to chair a board on reorganization of bureaus for a little while. The board recommended against combining the Bureau of Ordnance and Bureau of Aeronautics, but it was done later.

Every Secretary of the Navy in the world, as near as I can figure, when he took over the job, immediately set out to reorganize the Navy

---
[*]Vice Admiral Robert P. Briscoe, USN.
[**]Admiral Robert B. Carney, USN, CNO from August 1953 to August 1955.
[***]Vice Admiral Matthias B. Gardner, USN.

Department. Charlie Thomas was no exception. The first thing Charlie Thomas did, after he picked Arleigh Burke to be Chief of Naval Operations (which was one of the smartest moves he ever made, there was no question about that), was to put the heat on Arleigh Burke to get rid of "Wu" Duncan.* Admiral Duncan had been vice chief for some time and knew more about the Navy Department than the whole Navy Department ever knew in its whole career. Wu Duncan's approach to the Secretary was always pretty much the same. He said, "Now look. Before you kick the Navy Department apart, I urge you to find out two things. First, find out what the organization is, and then find out how it got that way, and why. Then after you kick it to pieces and you find that it doesn't work, you can put it back together again the way it was." That was Wu's advice to the Secretary and very sound advice it was, too.

Charlie decided that Wu was an old fud and that he had to be relieved. I'm sure Arleigh didn't want to relieve him; Arleigh wanted to keep him. I first ran into Wu Duncan when he was Admiral King's aviation operations officer shortly after the war. Doolittle's Tokyo raid was Wu Duncan's idea, and Wu Duncan was about as smart as they come. Admiral King had the highest regard for him. Wu was a rather quiet, unassuming gentleman, but he knew his stuff. He knew more about the Navy Department than anyone else ever did.

When Charlie Thomas became Secretary of the Navy and Tom Gates was the Assistant Secretary, I believe at the time, the first thing that

---
*Admiral Donald B. Duncan, USN, Vice Chief of Naval Operations, 1951-1956.

Charlie did was to set up a board to examine the reorganization of the Navy, which is, as I say, par for the course.[*] Tom Gates was on the board and John Dillon, who was the administrative officer.[**] John Dillon started off as a Marine sergeant sitting outside Secretary Knox's door and ended up being one of the top administrating officers in the Navy. A very competent guy. Johnny Gingrich was on it, and I was on it, Wu Duncan was on it.[***] We used to meet aboard the Secretary's yacht down at the gun factory.[****] We recommended, as I recall, very little in the way of reorganizing the Navy, but it's a hardy perennial.

When I came back after having been relieved as commander Battleships Cruiser Force Atlantic, I spent a couple of months heading this board to determine whether or not we should merge the Bureau of Aeronautics and the Bureau of Ordnance. We recommended against it at the time. It was eventually done by a later board.[*****] Now, of course, what has happened, if you've followed it, is that with unification, the office of the Secretary of Defense has expanded to the point where it's out of all possible managerial size--to where it

---

[*]Thomas S. Gates, Jr., was Under Secretary of the Navy, 1953-1957; Secretary of the Navy, 1957-1959; and Secretary of Defense, 1959-1961.
[**]Dillon was later given the job of reviewing the Navy's management system under Secretary of Defense Robert S. McNamara in 1962. The Dillon Board recommended unifying the "producer" bureaus into Chief of Naval Material and otherwise retaining the customary bilinear structure.
[***]Rear Admiral John E. Gingrich, USN.
[****]What used to be known as the Naval Gun Factory is now called the Washington Navy Yard.
[*****]The two were merged on 1 December 1959 to constitute the Bureau of Naval Weapons.

is simply a suffocating bureaucracy. What they have forced on the Navy is a bastardized organization which parallels that of the Army and Air Force. Now you have commands, such and such a command; you've got infinitely more people on the staff than you ever had before not doing any different than they ever did before but nobody knows. It now parallels the organization of the Army and the Air Force. In my opinion, it has the great advantage which the Army has thrived under all its career. It's an approach to the general staff system, and that means that you can never, under any circumstances, hold anybody responsible for anything. It's a great setup, but it isn't doing the Navy any good. You've got admirals all over the place. You've got a four-star admiral who is Chief of Naval Material--I don't know what they are, but the organization is just completely unwieldy. The Chief of Naval Operations now commands nothing; his flag is split down the middle; he's got a blue half and a white half which indicates that he's either in command of everything or I don't know what. It's out of this world as far as making any sense is concerned.

Q: At least when you were on the board you had the satisfaction of having them accept your recommendations.

Admiral Libby: They were temporary. I could see that Charlie Thomas was unhappy. I could see that he didn't like it, but he did approve it. It never got very far and almost immediately after we turned in our report, I went down to relieve Bobby Briscoe as OP-03. They started to set up another board which a few years later ended up with the merging of the two bureaus.

I was OP-03 only very briefly, and then Charlie Thomas's campaign to get rid of Wu Duncan came to fruition and then the question of who was going to be vice chief came to the fore. We were consulted, and we all made our recommendations. Matt Gardner hoped that he might get it, and when he didn't get it, he put in for retirement. So I took over his job, OP-06, instead of OP-03, which I retained until '58 when I came out to be commander of the First Fleet.

There again there was nothing of earth-shaking importance, just the usual routine, the usual battle for the budget. One of the most significant things that happened during that period, '56-'58, was the development of the Polaris submarine. Red Raborn was put in charge of developing the Polaris submarine.* He had to deal initially with the Redstone missile, which was produced by the Redstone Arsenal down in Huntsville, Alabama. It was liquid propelled and it's never been a great success. Some Army bloke, head of Army Research, remarked one day that he did not regard any missile with an apogee of five feet as being a great success.

Anyway, it became apparent early on that fuming nitric acid and liquid oxygen and liquid hydrogen were not compatible with the insides of a submarine. So Admiral Raborn persuaded Charlie Thomas to let him drop the Redstone and go ahead with solid propulsion, which he did. Charlie agreed to do it and the Polaris missile has been a

---
*Rear Admiral William F. Raborn, Jr., USN.

tremendous success all the way down the line and probably our most important deterrent today.

I didn't have any active part in developing this except to fight with the then vice chief who said we shouldn't mess with it, we should leave it up to the Air Force. I didn't quite agree. The Navy didn't need Polaris, but Polaris needed the Navy, so the country finally got it.

That was Don Felt who made a tremendous hit with Secretary Thomas.* He had a rather meteoric rise. He came into the Navy Department as one of the boys on the R&D section, as a rear admiral, in '56.** He immediately got promoted to vice admiral and went over and took command of the Sixth Fleet, and Charlie Thomas went over to visit the Sixth Fleet and came back and promptly made him vice chief, so he went from two stars to four stars in about five months.

Q: Did you not become a vice admiral during this period?

Admiral Libby: I became vice admiral when I became OP-06; when I left BatCruLant I was promoted to three-star admiral. Thanks to my good friend Arleigh Burke who shook the Navy by being made Chief of Naval Operations over several other people. But, as I see it, that was one of the smartest things Charlie Thomas ever did. I think it was too

---
*Admiral Harry Donald Felt, USN, whose oral history is in the Naval Institute collection. In April 1956 he was promoted to vice admiral when he became Commander Sixth Fleet. In September of that same year he received his fourth star when he relieved Admiral Duncan as Vice Chief of Naval Operations.
**R&D--research and development.

bad that the major advantage in that was vitiated by keeping him there for six years. What had happened in the CNO bracket was that the Class of '16 had passed the top jobs out among themselves for years and hadn't realized that the calendar had overtaken them. Arleigh, himself, told me during his last two years he never should have stayed more than four years. He wished he hadn't.

Q: Then as commander, First Fleet, I'm sure there are some incidents that you should relate during those two years.

Admiral Libby: I just came out here. I didn't even have a flagship. We were so short of ships in those days that I simply set up my shop over here on North Island, and we just carried out the routine training assignments with such ships as we had that came back from the Seventh Fleet. There was nothing of the slightest importance during that period.

Q: And you retired May 1, 1960. I'd like to have you tell me what your activities have been as a civilian.

Admiral Libby: I have written articles for the Copley News Service.*
At least I have until the present moment. How much longer I will

---

*The Copley News Service is a worldwide newsgathering organization owned by the Copley Press. Its owner, James Copley, is a philanthropist who in 1961 won the Military Order of World Wars National Gold Medal for his contributions to government.

continue to do so I don't know. The last three have been on the cutting room floor.

Q: Do they not like your outspoken comments?

Admiral Libby: I don't know. They haven't published the last three. I don't know why. Perhaps they're having a change of policy, or something. Some of them have been a little rough, I will admit. Maybe they're just being politic. When it became known that I was about to retire, Jim Copley asked me if I would undertake the job of writing articles for them on international affairs. I'd never done anything like that before, but I decided I would take a whirl at it, and I did. It's been very interesting. I've done a lot of traveling in that capacity. I've been to the Near East and the Far East, and around the world once, to Africa three times.

Q: I know that you are a public speaker of some note in the area.

Admiral Libby: I don't know how much note. Every now and then they put the arm on me and I have to go out and yack to them.

Q: Are you interested in politics?

Admiral Libby: I'm interested, but I don't take any active part in local politics, because it's not compatible with the Copley News

Service to take an active part in local politics. I have written some rather potent articles in favor of Mr. Nixon and in favor of what he's trying to do and I've taken our dove senators to pieces, if possible, on a number of occasions, without much success in getting it into print, I will admit. They were a little cautious, perhaps. I can understand that, because the Copley News Service services a lot of papers which are not strictly--they have to be nonpartisan up to a point, I'm quite sure. It's difficult to do. I'm so desperately concerned over what's happened to the country that I don't see much future.

Looking back on what's happened in the past 25 years, our defeated enemies are now our friends, and our erstwhile allies are now our avowed enemies. They are following a program for destroying the country--it's following right down the line, right down the blueprint, exactly what Lenin told them to do. It's not so hot.

Q: What do you consider your greatest contribution to your country during the years you were on active duty?

Admiral Libby: I don't think I made any great contributions at all. I just did my job to the best of my ability--no more contribution than any other naval officer and not as much as most. I had a very unspectacular career, let's put it that way.

Q: I want to review your contacts with Admiral King hoping we can get

Libby #4 - 220

some pictures of him that maybe the Institute doesn't have and we'll start with September 4, 1941 when you reported to him at the time when he was Commander in Chief of the Atlantic Fleet.

Admiral Libby: I had been over in England for almost a year, and I got dispatch orders to come back and report to King's staff—he was then Commander in Chief, U.S. Atlantic Fleet, and the flagship was the <u>Augusta</u> in Newport. I came back and got debriefed, as the Army says, in Washington for a few days and then went up and reported to his staff as assistant operations officer. By assistant, I mean assistant. I was just one of the boys in the back room. We had a little compartment that was the operations office and Captain "Frog" Low was the operations officer, "Tex" McLean was there and Harry Sanders was there, I was there, Oscar Badger was the chief of staff.*

The Atlantic Fleet was pretty much on the war status by then, even though Pearl Harbor had not happened. We were busy boys. I remember that Oscar Badger stuck his head in one day. We were all in the compartment where we didn't have any more room than we have on this table and he said, "My God, what a can of worms." And it was.

That was the first time I had ever served with Admiral King, and I must say frankly having come back from wartime England, I was a little terrified of the admiral. He had a reputation of being pretty grim,

---

*Captain Francis S. Low, USN; Commander Heber H. McLean, USN; Lieutenant Commander Harry Sanders, USN; Captain Oscar C. Badger, USN. A photograph of Admiral King's 1941 Atlantic Fleet staff, including names and ranks of the staff members, appears on page 58 of the August 1974 issue of the <u>U.S. Naval Proceedings</u>.

pretty rough. Which reputation, I must say, was entirely unjustified, but it sure took me some time to find out from whence it came. As I'm sure I've said before, his modus operandi was abysmally simple--he would give a man a job to do and give him everything he could give him to do the job with and let him severely alone. He wouldn't breathe down the back of his neck or tell him how to do the job, or have to be told every 20 minutes how he was doing. He would let him severely alone, and if the man did his job he would give him another one. If the man didn't do his job, he'd get rid of him and it's the people that he got rid of that went around saying what a SOB Admiral King was. It's just as simple as that.

Q: I have a couple of incidents that I wonder if you were aware of his reaction to them and also I want to refer to his book, which is a large volume, and it tells many things of Admiral King, but it somewhat tells what he did without telling how he felt or how he might have personally reacted, and that's what I would like to get from you if possible. For example: actually just a few days after you reported, on September 4th, the U boats attempted to torpedo the Greer. And then on October 15th, the Kearny was torpedoed and made it to port. October 30th the Reuben James was torpedoed and it sank with more than 100 casualties. Were you in a position to reflect Admiral King's reaction to those?

Admiral Libby: No, I wasn't close enough to him to know. I was an

Libby #4 - 222

assistant operations officer, pretty well down the echelon. We almost never saw him during that period. We were low men on the totem pole, really. His reaction, of course, would have been expressed to his chief of staff and other people, but we never got any particular--I can say this knowing him as I came to know him later, that he would have been quite unperturbed. I don't mean that he was in any way heartless, but he knew perfectly well that we were at war, as far as we were concerned. The Atlantic Fleet had been at war for some time, ever since the "neutrality patrol" was instituted. He would merely accept this as a casualty of war. He would not push the panic button, or anything else, I'm sure of that. He would just accept it as a matter to be expected.

Q: Now go on to Pearl Harbor.

Admiral Libby: Then came Pearl Harbor and shortly thereafter he told me to pack a suitcase, we were going down to Washington. We went down and he then told me he was going to be Commander in Chief, U.S. Fleet. That was really when the beginning of my close association with Admiral King started. For some time, he and I, just the two of us down there, functioned as Commander in Chief, U.S. Fleet because he didn't have any other staff. We had a beat-up, grimy old office on the third or fourth deck of the old Navy Department, and then he began to assemble his staff and began to operate at CominCh. He changed the name from CinCUS, which after Pearl Harbor he didn't think was very acceptable, to CominCh. During this period of time, the British Chiefs of Staff Committee came over, and Mr. Churchill came over and the U.S. Joint Chiefs of Staff came into being by virtue of necessity. I sort of became his secretary for JCS and Combined Chiefs of Staff matters, and at that point I became his aide for this purpose. Then he and I worked very closely together for some time.

Q: Where was your office in relationship to his?

Admiral Libby: Right outside his main office. He had a main office and an anteroom; I was in the anteroom. His flag lieutenant was Charlie Lanman.* I was just on one end of the squawkbox.

Q: So you saw him every day?

Admiral Libby: Yes, I talked to him every day from then until March of '43 when I got detached and went out to sea, so I was with him day and night for a long time.

Q: The visit of Winston Churchill was given the code name of Arcadia and you sat in on those conferences, I'm sure.

Admiral Libby: Oh, yes. Winston Churchill arrived with what the British call their Chiefs of Staff Committee just before Christmas

---
*Lieutenant Charles B. Lanman, USN.

1941. Of course, he holed up at the White House, and most of his staff were put up there. We started meetings with the British which soon became known as the Combined Chiefs of Staff over at the Public Health Building on Constitution Avenue, directly across the street from the old Navy Department. As I recall it, Beetle Smith was the secretary of what became the Joint Staff.* Mr. Roosevelt, Mr. Churchill, the British and ourselves started mapping a grand strategy of the war.

The first thing that was arrived at was called CCS-1, Combined Chiefs of Staff 1, that the defeat of Germany was the number one priority. Once Germany was defeated, Japan would automatically go down the drain perforce. I presumed there wasn't any other political way of arriving at anything. I mean it would have been politically impossible to arrive at any other conclusion, so that was adopted as the grand strategy of the war.

Q: Do you know whether Admiral King had any personal reservations on this matter?

Admiral Libby: I'm quite sure he did, as became evident later on when we had increasing difficulty getting anything at all out of the British to fight the Japs in the Pacific and when we were getting our nose rubbed in it pretty badly in the Pacific. But there it was, and we were stuck with it. I'm sure that Admiral King would have

---
*Walter Bedell Smith, named U.S. Secretary of the Combined Chiefs of Staff in February 1942.

preferred to have a little more leeway, a little more stuff to operate in the Pacific with, but he couldn't get it as a result of this CCS-1 which had been agreed to.

Q: Can you describe a typical day in Admiral King's office?

Admiral Libby: I don't know as there were any typical days. We were there seven days a week from 7:00 o'clock in the morning until midnight, depending on what was going on, and there was a lot going on. In addition to coping with the British visit and trying to get things organized and get the U.S. Navy operating on a war footing, and meeting with all the other boards and whatnot that Admiral King had to attend, such as the War Production Board, the Combined Allocations Committee, and this, that, and the other, he had the sizable job of setting up a staff. He had to get enough staff to run the Navy with. He had to scratch around and get people to come in. He brought them in from all over the place, I must say. I must also say that he had the most uncanny knowledge of people in the Navy of any man I ever heard of. He brought in people from everywhere around, and as far as I could see, every one of them topflight people. He knew the people he wanted, and he was in a position where he could get them.

Q: His book indicates that he liked to keep in touch with the fleet, to not get the Washington atmosphere and that he changed his staff quite frequently for that purpose.

Admiral Libby: He did. He brought in (I mentioned Wu Duncan)---everybody that he brought was just absolutely outstanding.

Q: You found him easy to work for?

Admiral Libby: Good Lord, yes. The most wonderful man to work for I've ever served in my life. He was marvelous.

Q: Was his disposition calm? Did he get mad?

Admiral Libby: Oh, he'd get mad occasionally, but who doesn't? He never got mad unless he had occasion to get mad.

Q: According to the people I hear speak of Admiral Nimitz, no one ever seems to have seen him get mad except maybe on one occasion, which is hard to believe.

Admiral Libby: I've never seen Admiral Nimitz lose his temper, but I knew he got mad. There's a difference. Ernie would occasionally blow his top; I never saw Admiral Nimitz blow his top, yet he could get just as mad as anybody else.

Q: Do you remember any of the matters over which Admiral King did blow his top?

Admiral Libby: Yes. This is one international incident where he really got angry and showed it. This was at the Casablanca Conference. He finally came flat out. The British and Mr. Churchill and company were so obviously wrapped up in the war in Europe, and trying to help Joe Stalin out, that the Pacific was obviously being completely ignored. Finally, he didn't pound the table, but he really got very emphatic. In effect he said, "When the Germans are defeated, are the British or are they not going to give us any help against the Japanese?" He put it right up to Winston Churchill, and he was obviously very angry about it. He felt he was getting the brushoff in the Pacific and, in effect, he was. You rarely see Mr. Churchill stopped, but he was stopped, and he gave the admiral assurance that the British would help us out against the Japs in the Pacific when Germany had been defeated.

Q: That's one of the occasions where you remember him being at least emphatic.

Admiral Libby: Oh, yes. I remember it very well and it had the desired effect, too, because the mighty Mr. Churchill took notice.

Q: Did he ever get mad or bawl out his subordinates?

Admiral Libby: I never heard him except personally--he used to read me off occasionally for matters which were eminently well deserved.

Never anything serious. I would make some blooper or other, and he would let me know that he didn't approve.

Q: He was a lonely man, wasn't he?

Admiral Libby: I don't think so. He'd be no more lonely than a man in a very high position has to be. He decided early on that he had to have a flagship, that he couldn't just live up at Quarters A there. He was just about to become CNO as well as CominCh. Admiral Stark had gone to London and Admiral King put his family in Quarters A up there at the Observatory but he, himself, brought the Dauntless down, which was a converted yacht, nothing very luxurious.* But he tied that up down there at the gun factory and he lived aboard that.**

Q: How did he travel from the Navy Department down to the Navy Yard?

Admiral Libby: In his car.

Q: What did he think about sending Admiral Stark to London as Commander U.S. Naval Forces Europe?

Admiral Libby: I don't know. He was a very good friend of Admiral

---

*Admiral Harold R. Stark, USN, CNO from August 1939 to March 1942; Commander U.S. Naval Forces in Europe at London, 1942-1945.
**The Naval Gun Factory was at what is now known as the Washington Navy Yard.

Stark's, and he was always extremely loyal to Admiral Stark. I can judge only by his behavior. He never made any move to push himself into the job of CNO. That was more or less thrust upon him by President Roosevelt. He was personally (he never said this to me and I can't prove this), I'm convinced, outraged by the filthy deal that Admiral Stark got over Pearl Harbor and I know that he was a prime mover in getting Admiral Stark his DSM after the war, which is quite a feat because the court of inquiry that sat on Pearl Harbor came up with the recommendation that Admiral Stark should never again be entrusted with a position of high responsibility. He was given a position of high responsibility in England, though, and then he got a DSM, thanks to Admiral King.[*] Ernie was very, very loyal. I don't think Admiral King felt that Admiral Stark was any ball of fire as CNO, which I don't think he was either. Admiral Stark is still with us, still living, and I won't say anything at all in derogation of him, but I feel that he was such a hound for detail himself that he didn't turn enough over to his hired help. He tried to carry the whole load on his own back, and I think things got out of hand.

Q: But for example, Marshall, who was his opposite number, stayed and went on to ...

---

[*]Admiral King initially joined in the criticism of Admiral Stark but later changed his mind in recommending him for the Distinguished Service Medal (DSM). See Thomas B. Buell, Master of Sea Power: A Biography of Fleet Admiral Ernest J. King (Boston: Little, Brown and Company, 1980), pages 351-353.

Admiral Libby: Well, Marshall obeyed orders. I'm absolutely convinced, and I will go to my grave convinced, that FDR ordered Pearl Harbor to be let happen. He must have known. He knew perfectly well that the Japs were going to attack us somewhere. All signs pointed to the fact that it was going to be at Pearl Harbor. They got the warning. General Marshall disappeared that Sunday moring and couldn't be found. He was riding at Fort Myer. Now if the Chief of Staff of the Army can't be found when he's riding a horse at Fort Myer on Sunday morning, there's something screwy somewhere. The warning was sent out by Western Union Telegraph on Marshall's orders, instead of picking up the telephone and calling General Short and calling Admiral Kimmel and saying, "Look boys, brace yourselves."[*] You can't kid me that General Marshall was not up to his ears in this. I am convinced that he had flat orders as to what to do from Mr. Roosevelt, and he did it.

Q: Did you ever hear Admiral King speak to that point?

Admiral Libby: No. He had too much sense. He never talked about it to me.

Q: He couldn't comment on it from his position.

---

[*] Lieutenant General Walter Campbell Short, AUS, commanded the Hawaiian Department between February and December 17, 1941; Admiral Husband Edward Kimmel was Commander in Chief of the Pacific Fleet from February 1941 to 17 December 1941.

Admiral Libby: Certainly not. All the voluminous investigations were a snow job.

Q: Do you think history will ever, even 100 years from now, reveal the truth?

Admiral Libby: I think the truth will eventually come out. I think it will have to.

Q: Do you have any information that would help historians?

Admiral Libby: I don't have any information at all. Everything I know is in the public domain. I can draw certain conclusions from it, as I think any intelligent person will have to draw. I just can't see it. Look at the logic of it. Admiral Stark was certainly no more to blame for Pearl Harbor than General George Marshall was. He couldn't have been. It was then the responsibility of the United States Army to defend Pearl Harbor, and the Army didn't do it. The only culpability that Admiral Kimmel could possibly have was (a) failure to work closely enough with General Short, which apparently he didn't do--he and Short were not on good terms, and (b) agreeing to base the fleet in Pearl Harbor.

Q: But he didn't have a choice on that.

Admiral Libby: He did, too. Admiral Richardson said, "I will not keep the fleet in Pearl Harbor—it isn't safe."* And he was relieved.

Q: You mean Admiral Kimmel should have done the same thing?

Admiral Libby: Admiral Kimmel should have said, "This isn't a safe place. I won't do it." He didn't do it, anyway.

Q: He was following orders.

Admiral Libby: Oh, sure, he was following the policy. He apparently thought it was safe, but he wasn't as bright as Admiral Richardson. Admiral Richardson said, "This is no place to keep the fleet, it's defenseless. The Army can't do anything about it; it isn't a safe place to base the fleet." And he wouldn't accept the responsibility. As for whether General Marshall was acting under orders—he must have been. There isn't any other way you can rationalize what happened. The things that he did and the things that he didn't do the morning of the 7th of December in Washington—if he hadn't been acting under the direct instructions from the Commander in Chief, he could not conceivably have hung onto the job of Chief of Staff of the Army. He could not possibly have done it. And the fact that nobody ever pointed a finger at him, no investigating committee ever indicated that he was in any way to blame—why should they nail Admiral Stark's

---
*Admiral James O. Richardson, USN, Commander in Chief U.S. Fleet, January 1940 until relieved in February 1941.

hide to the barn door and let Marshall go scot free and smelling like a rose if he wasn't doing what he was told?

So I say I'm not competent to judge whether Roosevelt was wise in doing this or not, but he certainly got the country united behind him. He was not confronted with what Mr. Nixon is facing today, and maybe it was a smart thing to do, I don't know. Maybe it saved lives in the long run, I don't know. Anyway, I'm convinced that's what happened. I don't think there's any other possible interpretation.

Q: Of course, we'll all be dead when the truth is revealed, if it is revealed, and it won't make any difference to those living then.

Admiral Libby: I think the truth is already revealed. It just isn't recognized. It's there for anybody to see; all you have to do is read the record. America likes to kid itself. There are certain myths which the American public takes unto its bosom and you couldn't shake them loose with a charge of dynamite. One of them being that Admiral Rickover developed the nuclear submarine over the dead bodies of every naval officer in the country.* There isn't a shred of truth in it, but that's what the American public believes. They'll never believe anything different.

Q: That is what I believe based on what I read.

---
*Rear Admiral Hyman G. Rickover, USN.

Libby #4 - 234

Admiral Libby: You believe that?

Q: I can only say that that is what is in the public press.

Admiral Libby: You don't believe it, do you?

Q: I don't know. Tell me different. Of course, I don't believe it, because I know other naval officers are concerned for their country's welfare and as competent. Maybe not as tough or as ...

Admiral Libby: The first concept of nuclear power, nuclear propulsion, in the Navy of which there is record was produced by two civilian scientists down at NRL in Anacostia. Somebody by the name of Gunn and somebody by the name of Abelson, two civilian scientists.* It was pushed by the Bureau of Ships. The best documentation of this thing that I could refer you to is one of Charlie Lockwood's latest books. I think it was <u>Down to the Sea in Subs</u>.** One of the last two or three that he wrote. He has it down there in black and white. Admiral Nimitz was interested in the nuclear submarine—he pushed it; a great many officers pushed it. As far as Admiral Rickover being the father of the submarine, it just isn't true. The American public

---
*Dr. Ross Gunn was Superintendent of Naval Research Laboratory's Division of Mechanics and Electricity from 1933-1947; Dr. Philip Abelson was noted for his discovery of neptunium. As a team they contributed to the success of the atomic bomb program and had been working on atomic propulsion when Rickover began his work.
**Vice Admiral Charles A. Lockwood, USN(Ret.), <u>Down to the Sea in Subs</u>, (New York: N.W. Norton and Company, 1967).

believes this to be the case because of somebody named Clay Blair, Jr., who was a *Time* correspondent in Washington at the time that Admiral Rickover was first passed over for selection from captain to rear admiral.* He said, "I know that Rickover was not selected, I know why perhaps he shouldn't be selected, but I'm warning you right now I can blow this up into another Dreyfus case.** This will sell magazines and I'm telling you from now on Admiral Rickover is my meal ticket." And he took it from there. Rick is a classmate of mine. I've known him all my life. He's a competent engineer, but that's all. He's no genius and he did not develop the nuclear-powered submarine over the resistance of every officer in the Navy. There isn't a single word of truth in it---not one solitary shred of fact.

Quite the contrary. When Earle Mills was Chief of the Bureau of Ships, the then Commander Rickover had the electrical design section in the Bureau of Ships.*** Earle Mills ordered him down to Oak Ridge to learn something about atomic power and Hymie didn't want to go. He fought it tooth and nail. He thought he was being sidetracked. Earle Mills finally told him, "You go down there and take this job or you

---

*Clay Blair, Jr.'s book on Admiral Rickover is *The Atomic Submarine and Admiral Rickover* (New York: Henry Hold and Company, 1954).

**Alfred Dreyfus, a French army officer, was indicted in 1894 for high treason on the charge of having authored a letter indicating the betrayal of military information to Germany. "L'Affaire" was a landmark in the history of France, resulting in intense internal divisions and a renewal of anti-Semitism. The case against Dreyfus was later dropped. Admiral Rickover also came from a Jewish background.

***Vice Admiral Earle W. Mills, USN, Chief of the Bureau of Ships from 1946 to 1949.

retire. Carry out your orders." Hymie went but practically over his dead body. That's how different fiction is from fact.

We have the same thing in Pearl Harbor. The American public will always believe that Kimmel and Short were to blame because they didn't do their job and therefore that their punishments were eminently justified.

Q: Of course, there's a lot of material being written that implies, but not to the same extent that you do, about Roosevelt.

Admiral Libby: You can't possibly arrive at any other conclusion if you look and see what happened that Sunday morning.

Q: When you were outside his office in the early days of 1942 when Halsey was making his raids on Wake Island, there were quick raids on Salamaua and Lae. Can you remember Admiral King in those early days of 1942 when this was taking place---his reactions?

Admiral Libby: We were just fighting a war. It was just a matter of daily routine. He was operating through Admiral Nimitz. They had certain strategic objectives--to hold the line as far forward as they could hold it and to keep the Japs as much off balance as they could with the shoestring forces we had. He left the detail of the operation up to Admiral Nimitz. As Commander in Chief, U.S. Fleet and as a member of the Joint Chiefs of Staff, the JCS would map out the overall strategy but the details, the daily operation, they left up to the operating commanders of the Pacific.

Q: Did he personally approve the Tokyo raid?

Admiral Libby: Yes.

Q: Do you remember the incidents surrounding that?

Admiral Libby: I didn't know anything about it until it was over. This was suggested by Wu Duncan, and it was all very hush-hush. We, in the lower echelon, didn't know anything about it until after it had taken place. Matt Gardner knew about it, Wu Duncan dreamed it up, Doolittle was in on it, because it was the B-25s that did it.* It was a very spectacular thing but as far as accomplishing any military objective, it was peanuts, though it was certainly a wonderful psychological blow to the Japs.

Q: And a wonderful psychological uplift to the Americans.

Admiral Libby: That's right. As I say, Wu Duncan was responsible for that. It was his idea. Admiral King told me after it was all over that it was Commander Duncan's idea. He said, "I like the way that boy thinks."

---
*Lieutenant Colonel James H. Doolittle, U.S. Army Air Forces.

Q: Do you ever remember Admiral King being particularly delighted over anything?

Admiral Libby: He was delighted over this.

Q: How did he react?

Admiral Libby: Just like anyone else would. He wasn't very demonstrative. You never knew particularly what he--he didn't jump up and down. He was under a terrific strain, of course, which he never particularly indicated. I think he was under far more of a strain than anyone actually realized. As you recall, we were taking an awful licking in the early days of the Pacific war. An awful lot of his friends and a lot of fine officers were getting killed, ships were being lost. We used to talk about the "calculated risk," one of his watchwords, and somebody out in SoPac said, "That's all very well.* Admiral King does the calculating and we take the risk." That got back to him, and that hurt him. I knew that he felt very badly about that, but there was nothing else he could do. He was carrying an awful load, and he was the only one in Washington that gave a damn about the Pacific at the time. Marshall couldn't care less, and the Army Air Corps boys didn't know which end was up. Admiral King was carrying the Pacific on his back with Nimitz's very capable help. Actually, until V-E Day, he was the only one in Washington who was

---
*SoPac--South Pacific.

really, and the only one among the Combined Chiefs of Staff, who was really paying attention to what went on in the Pacific.

Q: I know that he used to meet, at intervals, with Admiral Nimitz in San Francisco.

Admiral Libby: He used to fly out about once a month and meet with Nimitz in San Francisco.

Q: Were you always with him?

Admiral Libby: I only went with him once. George Russell used to go.* He generally took George Russell with him to the West Coast.

Q: I have read and heard a great deal about the intelligence at the time of the Coral Sea and the Midway battles and the problems that Admiral Nimitz had in convincing the people in Washington that the code, AF, where the attack was to come, was in fact Midway, and that many of the people in Washington, particularly the Army people, were convinced it was the West Coast. Do you remember any of the incidents involving that?

Admiral Libby: Your knowledge if far greater than mine. All I know about that is that we had broken the Japanese code before Midway, and

---

*Commander George L. Russell, USN, King's flag secretary.

we knew the attack was coming at Midway. We also knew considerable about the terrific forces that the Japanese had assembled for this thing. I don't know whether there was any disputation in Washington, or not, about it. I would not have been on it if there were. I also know it was a providential act that Bill Halsey got the shingles.* If Admiral Halsey had been in command, we would have lost the battle of Midway and all that was left of the U.S. Fleet. He would have been sucked in by the Japs.

Q: He would have gone chasing after them.

Admiral Libby: He certainly would have.

Q: There's some comment, I can't identify what book it was in, that the man who is credited with breaking, or reading the Japanese code, was recommended for the DSM and that Admiral King said no, he was doing what was his job.

Admiral Libby: That I don't know. I believe the code was broken by a cryptologist, Safford.**

Q: Safford was the boss of Rochefort.

---

*Vice Admiral William F. Halsey, Jr., USN.
**Captain Laurence F. Safford, USN.

Admiral Libby: I do know that some reporter on the Chicago Tribune got the word and blabbed it and the Chicago Tribune printed it, and Ernie really blew his top about that. That was one of the first things that got Admiral King completely soured on the press and on reporters during the war. He wouldn't give them the time of day if he could help it.

Q: It wasn't printed until afterwards, was it?

Admiral Libby: No, but anyway, the Japanese promptly changed their code immediately after the battle. That put us way back on page one. It was no easy matter to break that code. That put us back on the war effort for months. Ernie was very, very irate about the whole thing. I think Commander Seligman had something to do with it.* I think he told this reporter aboard the ship coming back from Midway in strict confidence that we had broken the Japanese code and the reporter printed it in the Chicago Tribune.**

Q: One questions what the definition of treason is almost, don't you?

Admiral Libby: Yes. Ernie was absolutely furious. It's a long time ago and I've forgotten the details, but I know that Ernie was just

---
*Commander M.T. Seligman, USN, executive officer of the carrier Lexington (CV-2), sunk in the Battle of the Coral Sea.
**For an account of this incident, see Robert Mason, "Eyewitness," U.S. Naval Institute Proceedings, June 1982, pages 40-45.

livid—he was absolutely burned up with fury over this one. I don't blame him at all.

Q: I have a feeling that Admiral King has been criticized for things that he may not have known about, that his staff members acted on and recommended to him. That's the way I would expect the size of that staff to have to ...

Admiral Libby: Probably, but Ernie knew a great deal about what was going on. He didn't miss much. There was very little that he didn't know. Nobody ever fooled him about anything, I'll tell you that. He was blessed with the God-given ability to pick smart people. Dickie Edwards, who became his deputy there, used to say he was president of the dead cat department.* Dickie Edwards took more load off Ernie King's back than any other ten men. He handled all the odds and ends and all the dirty political jobs around town, and he left Ernie free to fight the war. Richard Stanislaus Edwards—he was a whiz. Of course, "Savvy" Cooke, head of his planning office, had to be tops. Admiral Horne, who was his OP-04, head of the logistics—they were all people who were invaluable help to him.** But the point is, he knew who to get and he got them.

Q: That's probably the greatest criterion of greatness—knowing who

---

*Vice Admiral Richard S. Edwards, USN, King's chief of staff.
**Admiral F.J. Horne, USN, eventually Vice Chief of Naval Operations at the end of the war.

to get to work for you, which brings me to the point that you stayed with him a long time.

Admiral Libby: I was in a very, very minor capacity and I was only with him a little while.

Q: You were with him from the beginning of the war until March '43.

Admiral Libby: I was just one of the hired help. I'm talking about people in important positions who really could make or break him. He really picked top men.

Q: You told me about Admiral King's reaction in Casablanca. Do you have any other recollections of that conference?

Admiral Libby: I think he was as amused as I was at the complete inability of anybody to talk Lord Louis Mountbatten down. Lord Louis Mountbatten just got what he wanted by process of sheer physical exhaustion. He just wore everybody down. He commented on that one time--that was very unusual. Lord Louis was Chief of Combined Operations, in other words he was head of the commandos. As such, because of British law, he had to have a commission in the Army, the Navy, and the Royal Air Force. He generally wore his admiral's uniform, but he had a commission as a general in the Army and a marshal in the Air Force, as well as an admiral in the Royal Navy. He had to have these in order to run the combined operations. If he wanted something, they might just as well give it to him and save three hours of argument, because he would win out in the end. He could wear down Churchill; he could wear down anybody. That was quite evident there on one or two occasions.

Most of what was planned at Casablanca with respect to the Pacific never came off, which was too bad. It was one of the reasons Ernie got a little fed up with it, I think.

Q: And then a couple of months later, in March, you were detached and went out to the Pacific. Do you remember any of his parting words or advice to you?

Admiral Libby: Just the usual, good luck, good sailing. I had better correct the record. I said that Ernie used to read me out. He never did, really. He sometimes would look at me rather pityingly. I would feel about an inch high, but he never tore into me. He just pointed out my stupidities in a kind way.

Q: You speak of him with much admiration and even affection.

Admiral Libby: Good Lord, yes. I loved the man. As far as I was concerned, he was the greatest naval officer that ever lived. As I say, I came to work for him in fear and trembling, and there's no man on earth for whom I have a higher respect or love or admiration than I

have for him. Not anybody. He's really tops. A great man--a
wonderful man to work for and a wonderful man to be with.

Index to

Series of Taped Interviews

with

Vice Admiral Ruthven E. Libby, USN (Ret.)

Abner Read, USS (DD-526)
  This destroyer, damaged by a mine, was the only casualty of the Kiska invasion of August 1943, p. 94

Aeronautics, Bureau of
  Libby sits on board in the mid-1950s tasked with Navy Department reorganization that is against merging this bureau with Ordnance, but their recommendation is ignored, pp. 211, 213

Agriculture
  Libby sees plowing done by mules and camels while in Morocco for the 1943 Casablanca Conference, p. 70

Air Force, U.S.
  Upon formation by the National Defense Act in 1947, attempts to usurp Navy and Army roles in national defense, pp. 161-167; some in Navy felt missiles should be left to the Air Force in the mid-1950s, p. 216

Air Forces, U.S. Army
  Flew P-38s in Attu operation, p. 89; unconcerned with Pacific war, p. 238

Alanbrooke, First Viscount
  See Brooke, Alan F.

Aleutian Islands
  See Dutch Harbor; Attu; Kiska

Alexander, Lieutenant Commander Boyd R., USN (USNA, 1916)
  As commanding officer, faith in the agility of the USS Boggs (AG-19) causes him to leave his new automobile tires on the forecastle, which are ruined during target practice in the early 1930s, p. 36

Angaur
  Description of terrain, p. 132; landing in 1943 described as treacherous, p. 134

Army, U.S.
  Participation in beginnings of Joint Chiefs of Staff in 1942, pp. 56-57; participation in cold weather amphibious operation during Aleutian campaign, pp. 79-82; fights to retain role in Defense Department after formation of the Air Force in 1947, p. 163; responsibility for defense of Pearl Harbor in 1941, pp. 231-232

Attu
  U.S. Army troops trained in the desert for this early amphibious operation in 1943, and suffered for lack of warm clothing, pp. 79-82; command personnel for amphibious operation, pp. 83-84

Augusta, USS (CA-31)
    King and Libby aboard this cruiser when Pearl Harbor was
    attacked, pp. 5, 54

B-36
    Sought by the Air Force to enhance its strategic bombing
    capabilities in the late 1940s, pp. 162, 164; funds taken from
    the Navy's budget for this program, p. 165

"Battle of the Pips"
    Libby theorizes that the Japanese may have evacuated Kiska
    during this fruitless U.S. attack brought on by false radar
    echoes, p. 95

Battleship-Cruiser Force, U.S. Atlantic Fleet
    Deployment to Europe and the Mediterranean in the mid-950s, pp.
    209-210; with decommissioning of the last battleships in the
    mid-1950s, Libby's relief in this command had only cruisers, p.
    209

Bessell, Brigadier General William W., Jr., USA (USMA, 1920)
    As member of the Joint War Plans Committee towards the end of
    World War II, lit upon the 38th parallel as the division of
    responsibility between U.S. and Russians in Korea, pp. 142-143,
    145

Budget -- U.S. Navy
    Initially small budget cut even more in favor of the Air Force
    in late 1940s, p. 165

Blair, Clay, Jr.
    Time magazine correspondent who created notoriety concerning
    Rickover's career in the early 1950s, p. 235

Boggs, USS (AG-19)
    Libby characterizes duty on this target ship in the early 1930s
    as hard and monotonous, pp. 34-37; personnel in the early
    1930s, pp. 35-36

Bolte, Major General Charles, USA
    Flag officers Bolte and Libby take West Point's cadet aptitude
    test out of boredom in the late 1940s, and fail, pp. 175-176

Boone, Rear Admiral Joel T., MC, USN
    As chief of Joint Plans and Action Division in the Defense
    Medical Department, leaves position as a result of his
    criticism of planned closings of military hospitals in the late
    1940s, p. 164

Bradley, General Omar N., USA (USMA, 1915)
    As Chairman of the Joint Chiefs of Staff in early 1950,
    predicted no future for amphibious landings, pp. 162-163

Bremerton, USS (CA-130)
    Offered command of a battleship under construction, Libby turns
    it down to command this cruiser in 1946, p. 153; duties in the
    Western Pacific, p. 155; breaks anchor chain during storm in
    Hong Kong harbor, pp. 156-157

Britain
    Relations between top U.S. and British officers during World
    War II, p. 8; treatment of retired senior officers, p. 13; as
    assistant naval attache, Libby studies battle damage to London
    in the early part of World War II, pp. 50-51; living conditions
    for American military in late 1930s-early 1940s, pp. 51-52;
    British Army considered to be too lumbering, p. 67; load ship
    with oranges from Morocco during Casablanca Conference, pp. 70-
    71; disinterest in escorts for U.S. ships if it meant taking
    materiel from the combat effort, pp. 74-75; Libby hosts
    cocktail party in Hong Kong for British officers in the mid-
    1940s, pp. 157-158; see also Chiefs of Staff Committee;
    Combined Materials Allocation Committee; Churchill, Winston;
    Mountbatten, Lord Louis; Pound, Sir Dudley

Brooke, Alan F.
    As chief of the Imperial General Staff, antipathy to U.S.
    military leaders during World War II, p. 8

Burke, Arleigh A., USN (USNA, 1923)
    Requests relief from duty as U.S. delegate to Korean truce
    talks in 1952 out of frustration, pp. 181, 196; anecdote about
    Burke make 50 cents on sale of his electric blanket to Libby,
    p. 196; as Chief of Naval Operations, told by Navy Secretary
    Thomas to remove "Wu" Duncan, p. 212; Libby agrees with his
    selection as CNO, but feels he was in that position too long,
    pp. 212, 216-217

Burma
    Allied operation discussed and agreed upon at Casablanca
    Conference in 1942 never carried out, p. 73

Canada
    Base lease agreements regarding Labrador and Newfoundland in
    the late 1940s, pp. 172-174; see also Permanent Joint Board of
    Defense

Casablanca Conference (January 1943)
   French presence, p. 62; British presence, pp. 67, 71; accommodations for participants, p. 69; American presence, p. 71; security, pp. 71-72; decision to stop Murmansk convoys, p. 73; much of planning at conference never came about, pp. 73-74, 244; Burma operation discussed, p. 73; King confronts Churchill about joining the U.S. effort in the Pacific, p. 227; Mountbatten's success at conference, pp. 243-244

Chiefs of Staff Committee (Britain)
   Dealings with this joint service organization at the beginning of our involvement in World War II brought about the formation of our Joint Chiefs of Staff, pp. 56-57, 223-224

China
   General George Marshall's decision as Army Chief of Staff to pressure Russia into helping fight against the Japanese ultimately cost us China, pp. 147-148; inflated condition of Chinese economy in 1946-1947, pp. 153-154; at Korean War truce talks, pp. 185-186, 189

Churchill, Winston
   Attitude towards deGaulle, p. 63; presence at London Conference in 1942, p. 64; relations with Admiral Ernest King, p. 67; relations with FDR, pp. 68, 75-76; tiff with Churchill relegates General McNaughton back to Canada, p. 171; confronted by King at Casablanca Conference to assist fight against the Japanese, p. 227; relations with Mountbatten, p. 244

CinCUS
   See Commander in Chief, U.S. Fleet

Circular Fleet Formation
   Used by carrier task force on the way to Wake Island action in 1943, pp. 100-101

Clark, General Mark W., II, USA (USMA, 1917)
   As Commander in Chief, U.S. Command during Korean War, maintained good relations with U.S. negotiators, p. 192

Code Breaking
   See Intelligence

Cold Weather Operations
   Troops trained for Attu amphibious operations in desert and were ill-prepared for bitter cold, pp. 79-82

<u>Colorado</u>, USS (BB-45)
   Attacked with 5-inch guns by Japanese on Tinian in July 1944, pp. 124-125

Combined Chiefs of Staff (U.S.-British)
  Meetings held in Washington in 1941-1942 between British Chiefs
  of Staff Committee and newly-formed Joint Chiefs of Staff, pp.
  57-58; agreed to make defeat of Germany first priority, pp. 74, 224

Combined Materials Allocation Committee
  Admiral King unsuccessfully approaches this joint British-U.S.
  committee to request adequate supplies to keep Atlantic convoys
  in action, p. 75

CominCh
  See Commander in Chief, U.S. Fleet

Commander in Chief, U.S. Fleet (CominCh)
  Offices in old Navy Building in 1943, pp. 5, 54, 222; Admiral
  King changes acronym from CinCUS to CominCh after disaster at
  Pearl Harbor, p. 54; routine in early 1940s, p. 225

Communists
  Chinese and North Korean personnel at Korean War truce talks,
  pp. 185-186, 203; approach to negotiating and tactics, pp. 187-
  189, 194, 196-197, 199-201; wanted all their prisoners of war
  returned with no option for repatriation, p. 190; Western
  communist journalists, pp. 198-199

Concord, USS (CL-10)
  Battered by foul weather off Pacific coast during fleet
  exercise in the 1930s, pp. 40-41; difficulty while refueling
  from the New Mexico, pp. 43-44

Construction Corps--U.S. Navy
  Libby aroused by the ire of naval constructors in the mid-1920s
  by backing out of a postgraduate course in naval engineering,
  pp. 28-31

Cooper, Commander Joshua W., USN (USNA, 1927)
  As destroyer squadron commander, offers gunfire support to
  underwater demolition team personnel laying charges off beach
  at Palau in 1943, pp. 117-118; at Pelelieu operation, p. 136

Copley News Service
  Hires Libby after retirement from the Navy in 1960 to write on
  international affairs, pp. 217-219

Cooke, Vice Admiral Charles M., USN (USNA, 1910)
  Credited for part in brilliant Pacific war strategy as chief of
  staff to Admiral King, pp. 137-138, 242

Cruiser Division Three
  Operations during early part of Korean War, pp. 177-180

Cruiser Division 11 (CruDiv 11)
    Libby commands CruDiv 11 for four days before command dissolved
    in 1946, pp. 151-152

Dauntless, USS (PG-61)
    Chief of Naval Operations, Admiral Ernest King, lives aboard at
    the Washington Navy Yard during World War II, p. 228

David Taylor Model Basin
    A tour of this facility while training in naval construction
    convinces Libby to switch to sea duty, p. 29

Defense Department
    Overabundance of staffs in all services' organizations, pp.
    213-214; see also Johnson, Louis A.; Lovett, Robert A.; Wilson,
    Charles E.; McElroy, Neil H.; McNamara, Robert S.

deGaulle, General Charles
    As French officer in exile in Britain, cool to Admiral Ernest
    King upon their meeting in London in 1942, pp. 61-62; meeting
    with Vichy General Giraud in 1943, p. 62; position defended by
    U.S. general Wedemeyer, p. 63

Denfeld, Admiral Louis, USN (USNA, 1912)
    Assessed as Chief of Naval Operations by Libby, p. 161; fired
    in 1949, pp. 166-168; lack of interest in his Joint Chiefs of
    Staff position, p. 168

Destroyer Squadron One
    Participation in Aleutians campaign between April and September
    1943, pp. 81-95; escorts merchant ships from Dutch Harbor to
    Pearl Harbor, pp. 98-100; escorts carrier task force to Wake
    Island, pp. 100-103; escorts task force to the Gilbert Islands,
    pp. 103-106

Destroyer Squadron 56
    Participation in Marianas campaign off Saipan, pp. 107, 115-
    116, 118-122; destroyer, missing from position in formation,
    ends up being in wrong formation, p. 119; participation in
    Palaus action, pp. 116-118, 131-136

Dill, Clarence E.
    Oregon congressional representative gives his third alternate
    appointment for the Naval Academy to Libby in 1918, p. 21

Dodd, Brigadier General Francis T., USA (USMA, 1923)
    As officer in charge of captured Communists during the Korean
    War, taken by his prisoners and when released, demoted, p. 205

Doolittle Raid
    Idea credited to "Wu" Duncan, aviation operations officer to
    Admiral King's Commander in Chief, U.S. Fleet staff, p. 212;
    Admiral King's reaction to, p. 238

Duncan, Admiral Donald B. "Wu", USN (USNA, 1917)
    Fired at Navy Secretary Thomas's behest because he discouraged
    reorganization of the Navy Department in the mid-1950s, p. 212;
    assessed by Libby, p. 212; responsible for Tokyo raid during
    World War II, pp. 212, 237

Dutch Harbor
    Difficulty for ships caused by unusual weather conditions
    around island during fleet exercise in the 1930s, pp. 42-44

Early, Steve
    President Franklin Roosevelt's card-playing press secretary on
    the way to 1942 London Conference, pp. 60-61

Edwards, Vice Admiral Richard S., USN (USNA, 1907)
    His invaluable help as King's chief of staff was a credit to
    King's ability to choose officers, p. 242

Eisenhower, General Dwight D., USA (USMA, 1915)
    Protection given Eisenhower at Casablanca Conference, pp. 71-
    72; ordered to let Russians enter Berlin first after surrender,
    p. 146

Fairbanks, Lieutenant Douglas E., USNR
    Presence as landing craft commander at Attu, p. 86

Felt, Admiral Harry D., USN (USNA, 1923)
    Strong impression made on Secretary of the Navy Thomas leads to
    Felt's rapid rise in rank in 1956, p. 216

Ferenbaugh, Major General Claude B., USA (USMA, 1919)
    As U.N. negotiator at Korean War truce talks, expert at
    horseshoes, pp. 195-196

First Fleet
    Lack of ships in the late 1950s causes Libby to head fleet
    without flagship, p. 217

Flame throwers
    Use at Saipan invasion and throughout World War II, pp. 140-141

Fleet formations
    See Circular Fleet Formation

Fog
   Difficulties with during Attu operations in 1943, pp. 83-85; see also Foul Weather

Fort, Rear Admiral George H., USN (USNA, 1912)
   His staff as Commander Task Force 32 during Palau operation in late 1943, pp. 131-132

Foul Weather
   New Mexico and other ship participating in fleet problem battered off Pacific coast in late 1930s, pp. 40-41; in Bering Sea during Alaskan patrols, pp. 92-93, 97-98; during refueling in Bering Sea, pp. 93-94; effect on TBS, p. 105; in Mediterranean in the mid-1950s, pp. 209-210; see also Williwaw; Fog; Cold Weather Operations

France
   Difficulties for British and Americans caused by strident personality of General deGaulle, pp. 61-63; see also Giraud, General Henri H.

Fuel Oil
   Difficulty refueling between the Concord (CL-10) and the New Mexico (BB-40) in the mid-1930s, pp. 43-45

Gay, Commander Jesse B., Jr., USN (USNA, 1935)
   First lieutenant of the Bremerton saves the day in Hong Kong harbor by lowering second anchor when first breaks during storm in the mid-1940s, pp. 156-157

Germany
   Decided by Combined Chiefs of Staff, meeting in Washington in 1942, that Germany was first priority for war effort, pp. 58, 74, 224

Gilbert Islands Campaign (November 1943)
   Difficult escort duty for Destroyer Squadron One from Pearl Harbor to the Gilberts, p. 103; participation of Task Force 52.2, pp. 104-105; see Tarawa

Giraud, General Henri H.
   Vichy French general's meeting with deGaulle in Casablanca in 1943, p. 62

Griffin, Rear Admiral Robert M., USN (USNA, 1911)
   As Commander, Task Force 52.2, angered at Libby's suggestion that battleships lower gunsights during Gilberts action, pp. 104-105

Guadalcanal
  Used as practice target for amphibious landing on Pelelieu, p. 133; King realizes strategic importance of this then-unknown island, p. 138

Guam
  Conditions of Nimitz's Pacific Fleet headquarters on Guam compared to Hawaii, pp. 15-16

Gunfire support
  At Attu landing, pp. 85-86; difficulty off Holtz Bay in Aleutians, pp. 96-97; during Gilberts campaign, pp. 104-105; Libby develops doctrine for training at Pearl Harbor in 1944, pp. 111-115; at Pelelieu landing, pp. 134-135; during Korean War, p. 178

Gunnery practice
  Austere state of the Navy in 1920s precludes extensive practice, pp. 32-33

Halsey, Vice Admiral William F., Jr., USN (USNA, 1904)
  Libby sees it as fortunate that Halsey was incapacitated with shingles prior to battle of Midway, p. 240

Hawaii
  Libby sets up gunfire support training range on Kahoolawe island in 1944, pp. 111-112; see also Pearl Harbor

Helena, USS (CA-75)
  Cruiser Division Three flagship hits North Korean battery in Wonsan, p. 179

Helicopters
  North Koreans covet helicopters used by American delegation at truce talks, p. 184

Hong Kong
  Libby sent to Hong Kong in charge of clearing remnants of U.S. Navy from city in mid-1940s, pp. 155, 159-160; Bremerton breaks anchor chain during storm in Hong Kong Harbor, p. 156; Libby hosts cocktail party for British officers and is charged twice for his bill, pp. 157-159

Hopkins, Harry
  Fervent card-player as assistant to President Roosevelt on way to London Conference in 1942, pp. 60-61

Hsieh, Major General Fang
  Assessed as Chinese representative at Korean War truce talks, pp. 185-186, 189

Inflation
In China in 1946, pp. 153-154; in the United States in 1970, p. 154

Intelligence
Through code breaking, knowledge in Washington of planned Japanese attack at Midway, pp. 239-240

Italy
Fierce fighting during World War II in what was supposed to be "soft underbelly", p. 72

Jacoby, Lieutenant Commander Oswald, USNR
As member of Libby's prisoner of war delegation at Korean War truce talks, pp. 201-202

Japan
Effectiveness of Japanese mortars at Attu, p. 85; torpedo planes, mistaking destroyer *Phelps* for a cruiser, set torpedoes too deep, p. 90; use of submarines around Alaska in World War II, p. 96; ability to withstand preliminary bombardments because of good shelters and trenches, pp. 106, 108; submarines sunk off Marianas, p. 121; Japanese on Tinian chose to die rather than surrender to Americans, pp. 122-124; familiarity with South Pacific islands, pp. 138, 140; Joint War Plans Committee's plans for invasion of Kyushu precluded by atomic bomb, pp. 146-147

Johnson, Louis A.
As Defense Secretary in the late 1940s, worked with President Truman to build-up the Air Force and reduce the other services, pp. 163-166; fires CNO Denfeld and causes Navy Secretary Sullivan to resign in 1949, p. 167

Johnson, U. Alexis
Sent by State Department to Korean War truce talks to attempt to speed-up negotiations, p. 191

Joint Chiefs of Staff (JCS)
Formation at beginning of U.S. involvement in World War II patterned after British Chiefs of Staff Committee, pp. 56-57; involvement in Korean War, p. 192; strategic planning during World War II, pp. 236-237

Joint Intelligence Committee (JIC)
Conducted briefing for Joint Chiefs of Staff and other Washington staffs during World War II, p. 150

Joint Strategic Survey Committee (JSSC)
   Libby recollects that before the end of World War II this far-sighted strategy group recommended a strong line towards Russia as soon as the war ended, pp. 144-145

Joint War Planning Committee
   Libby receives citation as senior U.S. Navy member, pp. 76-77; personnel, pp. 77-78, 142; draws arbitrary line through Korea for dividing responsibility between the Soviet Union and the U.S. that becomes the infamous 38th Parallel, pp. 142-143, 145-146; plans invasion of Kyushu which is precluded by atomic bomb, pp. 146-147; concern with Battle of the Bulge, pp. 149-150; daily operations, pp. 150-151

Joy, Vice Admiral C. Turner, USN   (USNA, 1916)
   As Commander U.S. Naval Forces Far East in the early 1950s asks Libby to replace Arleigh Burke on Korean War truce talks team, p. 181; as U.N. negotiator, pp. 187, 193, 196-197; health worsened in Korea, p. 204

Kauffman, Rear Admiral James L., USN   (USNA, 1908)
   As Commander Destroyers Pacific Fleet during World War II, orders Libby to develop doctrine for close gun support training, p. 111

Kentucky, USS   (BB-66)
   Libby offered command of this battleship under construction, but turns it down for the USS Bremerton (CA-130) in 1946, p. 153

Kimmel, Admiral Husband E., USN   (USNA, 1904)
   Culpability for Pearl Harbor attack, pp. 230-232, 236

King, Admiral Ernest J., USN   (USNA, 1901)
   Selects Nimitz for Pacific Fleet command, pp. 1, 6; relationship with Nimitz, pp. 2, 9-10, 236, 238-239; ability to suit personnel to positions, pp. 3, 55, 225, 242; assessed by Libby, pp. 3, 221-222, 226, 228, 238, 242, 244-245; changes policy of supply corps regarding helpfulness to ships, p. 48; stern reputation, pp. 53, 220-221; kept separate his staffs for U.S. Fleet and Naval Operations, p. 55; relations with Churchill, p. 67; unsuccessfully sought materiel to keep Atlantic escorts in force, pp. 74-75; credited for brilliant Pacific war strategy, pp. 137-139; promotes Libby to commodore in mid-1940s, p. 142; U.S. Atlantic Fleet staff, p. 220; leadership methods, p. 221; reservations about decision with British to make Germany first priority, pp. 224-225; confronts Churchill about British assistance in fight against Japan, p. 227; living accommodations as CNO, p. 228; as show of loyalty

to Admiral Stark, pushes through a Distinguished Service Medal after the war, pp. 228-229; reaction to Doolittle Raid, pp. 237-238; angered at press leaks, especially about codebreaking before Midway, pp. 241-242; staff as CNO, p. 242; amused by Mountbatten's use of exhaustive argument to get what he wanted, pp. 243-244; see also Commander in Chief U.S. Fleet

Kinkaid, Rear Admiral Thomas C., USN (USNA, 1908)
As Commander, Northern Pacific Force during World War II, invites Libby to lunch where beer is served, p. 97

Kiska
Japanese had already evacuated by the time the U.S. invaded in August of 1943, p. 94; see "Battle of the Pips"

Knox, Frank
As Navy Secretary in the early 1940s, selects Nimitz as Commander, Pacific Fleet, pp. 1, 6

Korea
Joint War Plans Committee divides country along the 38th parallel towards the end of World War II to determine U.S. and Soviet responsibilities, pp. 142-143, 145-146; see also Korean War

Korean War
Timeliness for preserving U.S. Navy and Marine Corps missions against dissolvement, p. 165; Cruiser Division Three bombs Wonsan, pp. 177-179; carrier operations, pp. 179-180; description of site of truce talks at Panmunjom, pp. 182-185; personnel at truce talks, pp. 185-186, 188-189, 195; U.N. peace delegates harassed at initial meetings at Kaesong, pp. 196-197; U.S. delegation, p. 201; negotiations hampered by U.S. initiatives from Washington, pp. 192-193; see Prisoners of War; Helicopters

Landing Craft
Nine landing craft lost at Pearl Harbor while loading ammunition, p. 128; meticulous planning to have slower craft arrive at same time as bigger ships, p. 128

Lee, Major General Sang Cho
North Korean Army general who was Libby's equivalent in discussion of prisoners of war during Korean War truce talks, pp. 185, 188; retort to Lee by Libby draws attention from media, pp. 198, 200

LeMay, General Curtis E., USAF
As Air Force Deputy Chief of Staff in the mid-1950s, displays athletic prowess during seminar at Quantico, pp. 207-208

Leyte Gulf (October 1944)
　Palaus operations were a preparation for this landing, p. 132

Libby, Vice Admiral Ruthven E., USN (USNA, 1922)
　Family, pp. 26-28, 31-32, 51, 54; background to attending the Naval Academy, pp. 19-21; midshipman at Naval Academy from 1918-1922, p. 22; postgraduate course in naval construction, pp. 28-31; turret officer in USS Utah (BB-31) in mid-1920s, p. 31; duty in USS Colorado (BB-45) from 1926-1929, pp. 32-33; master's degree in electrical engineering, pp. 33-34; executive officer in USS Macdonough (DD-251) from 1937 to 1938, pp. 38-47; engineer officer in USS Northampton (CA-26) from 1938-1939, pp. 47-49; assistant naval attache in London from 1940-1941, pp. 50-52; assistant operations officer, staff of U.S. Atlantic Fleet Commander, pp. 220-222; aide to Commander in Chief, U.S. Fleet from 1941 to 1943, pp. 2, 5-11, 53-76, 222-245; Commander Destroyer Squadron One from 1943 to 1944, pp. 2, 78-106; Commander Destroyer Squadron 56, in 1944, pp. 107-111, 115-141; temporary assignment to staff, Commander Destroyers Pacific Fleet, pp. 111-114; senior naval officer on Joint War Planning Committee in 1945, pp. 77-78, 142-151; brief duty as Commander, Cruiser Division 11 in 1946, pp. 151-152; commanding officer, USS Bremerton (CA-130) from 1946 to 1947, pp. 153-160; chief of staff in 1947, pp. 160-169; as Director, General Planning Group, Naval Operations in the late 1940s, additional duty on Permanent Joint Board of Defense, U.S.-Canada, pp. 169-176; Commander, Cruiser Division Three from 1950-1952, pp. 177-180; Navy delegate on U.N. Korean War truce talks from 1952 to 1953, pp. 181-206; Assistant Chief of Naval Operations (Operations) from 1953-1954, pp. 206-208; Commander, Battleship-Cruiser Force, U.S. Atlantic Fleet from 1954-1956, pp. 209-211; Deputy Chief of Naval Operations (Fleet Operations and Readiness) from 1956-1958, pp. 211-217; Deputy Chief of Naval Operations (Plans and Policy) in 1956, on board studying reorganization of Navy Department, pp. 211-215; Commander, First Fleet, 1958-1960, p. 217; retirement from active duty in May 1960, p. 217; medals and decorations, pp. 76-77, 95-96, 141; retirement interests, pp. 217-219

Liscome Bay, USS (CVE-56)
　Disintegrates when hit by undetected Japanese torpedo near Makin in 1943, pp. 105-106

London Conference (June 1942)
　Personnel present, pp. 60-62, 64; social aspect, pp. 65-66; outcome, pp. 66-67

Lovett, Robert A.
　Description of negotiations with Communists as Deputy Secretary and Secretary of Defense in the early 1950s, p. 187

Macdonough, USS (DD-351)
  Rolling tendencies of this 1,500-ton destroyer, pp. 39, 41; personnel in mid-1930s, pp. 39, 46; participation in fleet exercise in Dutch Harbor, pp. 40-42, 45-46; commanding officer relieved after collisions, p. 84

McElroy, Neil H.
  As Defense Secretary in the late 1950s, continues his predecessor's practice of conducting seminars at Quantico, but makes them all business, p. 207

McNamara, Robert S.
  Assessed as Defense Secretary by Libby, pp. 165-166, 203-204

McNarney, General Joseph T., USAF (USMA, 1915)
  Air Force advisor to Defense Secretary Louis Johnson gives part of the Navy's budget to Air Force B-36 program, pp. 164-165

McNaughton, Andrew G.L.
  Assessment of Canadian chairman of the Permanent Joint Board of Defense in the late 1940s, pp. 170-172

McNeil, Wilfred J.
  As comptroller of the Defense Department in the mid-1950s, rooms with General LeMay during seminar at Quantico, pp. 207-208

Makin (November 1943)
  Loss of Liscome Bay, pp. 105-106; ineffectiveness of shore bombardment, pp. 106, 108; importance because of nearness to Japanese airfield, p. 109

Marianas Campaign (June - August 1944)
  Use of star shells in gunfire support, p. 115; weather conditions, pp. 126-127; see also Saipan; Tinian

Marine Corps, U.S.
  Anecdote showing enlisted Navy's unfamiliarity with Marine flag officers, pp. 87-88; marine captures 18 Japanese on Tinian in 1944, pp. 129-130; existence threatened by President Truman in 1950, p. 163; saved by Korean War, p. 165

Marshall, General George C., USA
  Concerned that Kwantung Army would never surrender, insisted that Russians got into fight versus Japan, which ultimately cost us China, pp. 124, 147-149; Libby speculates on role in Pearl Harbor attack, pp. 229-233; unconcerned with Pacific War, p. 238

Maryland, USS (BB-46)
  Anecdote about sailor working on cargo net-ladder for
  amphibious landings and a Marine Corps brigadier general, pp.
  87-88

Maury Prize
  Presented to Libby as a sophomore at the Naval Academy for
  excellence in physics, p. 23

Mediterranean
  Winter weather, pp. 209-210; lack of Russian presence in the
  early 1950s, pp. 210-211

Meiling, Dr. Richard L.
  Defense Department Director of Medical Services advocates
  closing of military hospitals in the late 1940s, p. 164

Merchant Ships
  As Commander, Destroyer Squadron One escorting merchant ships
  from Dutch Harbor to Pearl Harbor, Libby's difficulty getting
  them to darken their lights as a security precaution, pp. 98-99

Midway Islands
  Code breaking provided information on Japanese plans prior to
  an attack, pp. 239-242; story about planned attack and broken
  Japanese code runs in U.S. newspaper, p. 241; see Halsey, Vice
  Admiral William F., Jr., USN

Military Academy, U.S.
  Flag officers Libby and Bolte take the cadet aptitude test out
  of boredom and fail, pp. 175-176

Military Armistice Committee
  Rotation system of officers involved in Korean armistice,
  p. 195

Mills, Vice Admiral Earle W., USN (USNA, 1918)
  As Chief of the Bureau of Ships in the late 1940s has to order
  CDR Rickover, in the electrical design section of his
  department, to learn about atomic power, pp. 235-236

Monaghan, USS (DD-354)
  Chases Japanese submarine onto beach at Kiska during Aleutians
  campaign, p. 96

Montgomery, Rear Admiral Alfred E., USN (USNA, 1912)
  Insistence on flaghoisting his night orders as Commander Task
  Force 14 causes difficulties for Libby aboard the Phelps in
  1943, pp. 102-103

Morocco
   Farming in the 1940s, p. 70; oranges, pp. 70-71; see also Casablanca Conference

Mountbatten, Lord Louis
   Burma operation, planned at Casablanca Conference with Mountbatten in charge, never materializes, p. 73; ability to get what he wanted through exhaustive arguing evident at Casablanca, pp. 243-244

Mullinnix, Rear Admiral Henry M., USN (USNA, 1916)
   Lost in the torpedoing of the <u>Liscome Bay</u> in 1943, pp. 105-106

Murray, Colonel James C., USMC
   As U.N. command liaison officer during Korean War truce talks, tasked with investigating outlandish charges of U.S. misdemeanors, p. 199

Nam, General Il
   North Korean general assessed as representative to Korean War truce talks, pp. 185, 189

National Security Act, 1947
   Advent of the U.S. Air Force adversely affects the U.S. Navy, p. 161

Naval Academy, U.S.
   Attrition in the early 1920s, pp. 24-25; Navy allows graduates in the early 1920s to resign upon graduation because of surplus of ensigns, pp. 25-26; midshipman cruises to Europe in the mid-1950s, pp. 209-210

Naval Construction
   Libby opts for naval construction after academy graduation but becomes disenchanted and switches to sea duty, pp. 28-31

Naval Gunfire Liaison Officers
   Marine officers' duties during Attu operation, pp. 86-87

Naval Reservists
   Proliferation in Destroyer Squadron 56 during World War II, p. 110; training, p. 111

Navy Department
   Reorganization of department first goal of many new Secretaries, pp. 211-213; board instituted under Secretary Thomas to study reorganization in the mid-1950s, p. 213; see also Knox, Frank; Sullivan, John L.; Thomas, Charles S.

Navy of the 1920s
  Glut of ensigns causes Navy to allow Naval Academy graduates to leave without serving, pp. 25-26; lack of funds curtails gunnery drills, pp. 32-33; personnel, p. 33

New Mexico, USS (BB-40)
  Participation in fleet exercise in the Aleutians in the mid-1930s, p. 40; disastrous refueling, pp. 43-44

Newcomb, USS (DD-586)
  Used white phosphorus shells during gunfire support at Pelelieu in 1943, pp. 134-135; receives unit citation for participation in Saipan-Tinian, Palau, and Surigao Strait action, p. 141; see also Destroyer Squadron 56

News Media
  Coverage of Korean War truce talks, pp. 182-183; Communist correspondents, pp. 198-199; Admiral King angry with news leaks during World War II, especially concerning codebreaking before Midway, pp. 241-242

Nimitz, Fleet Admiral Chester W., USN (USNA, 1905)
  Sent by CNO King and Navy Secretary Knox to Pacific Fleet command, pp. 1, 5-7; relations with King, pp. 2, 9, 236, 238-239; built morale by personally welcoming back ships to Pearl Harbor, pp. 2-3, 18; ability to suit personnel to positions, pp. 3, 55; assessed by Libby, pp. 3, 14, 226; funeral in 1966, p. 3; family, pp. 4, 13; anger in defense of officer against King, pp. 9-10; great storyteller, pp. 3, 11-12; invited to move into Navy quarters in 1963, pp. 12-14; anecdote showing his dedication to duty, pp. 15-17; credited for brilliant Pacific war strategy, pp. 137-138

Norman Scott, USS (DD-690)
  Attacked with 5-inch gun by Japanese on Tinian in July 1944, pp. 124-125

Northampton, USS (CA-26)
  Characteristics assessed by engineering officer Libby, p. 47; relationships between department heads, p. 48; among first ships overhauled at Pearl Harbor in the late 1930s, p. 49

Nuclear Power
  Libby debunks myth of Rickover's singlehanded development of nuclear power over great objections, pp. 234-236

O'Donnell, Lieutenant Commander John J., USN (USNA, 1922)
  As first lieutenant on the Northampton in the late 1930s, friendship with classmate and chief engineer Libby overrides traditional antagonism of their positions, p. 48

Oil
  Difficulty refueling between the Concord (CL-10) and the New Mexico (BB-40) in the mid-1930s, pp. 43-45

Orange War Plan
  Libby sees strategy formulated after World War I as unworkable for situations encountered in World War II, p. 137

Ordnance, Bureau of
  Libby sits on board tasked with Navy Department reorganization that is against merging this bureau with Aeronautics, but their recommendation is ignored, pp. 211, 213

P-38
  Used by the Army Air Forces in the Aleutians campaign in 1943, p. 89

Pacific War
  At 1942 Casablanca Conference, Allies agree to give European war priority over Pacific, p. 66; King's discontent with lack of concern about Japan, p. 67; Pacific strategy defended by Libby, pp. 137-140; Doolittle Raid gives tremendous morale boost, pp. 237-238; see also Japan; Marianas Campaign; Aleutians Campaign; Wake Island; Palaus Campaign; Gilbert Islands Campaign; Savo

Palaus Campaign (September - October 1943)
  Closeness to beach of ships offering gunfire support, p. 116; naval personnel in charge, pp. 117, 131-132; underwater demolition team used on beach, pp. 117-118; operation rehearsed at Guadalcanal, p. 131; objectives, p. 132; narrow passage between Pelelieu and Angaur causes problems, p. 133; Libby defends strategy in this operation, pp. 137-140; see also Pelelieu; Angaur

Panmunjom, Korea
  Discussion of truce talks during Korean War, pp. 182-201

Patrol Duty
  Boredom of patrolling in Aleutians in 1943, p. 92

PBY (Catalina)
  Used to lead Army P-38s in bombing raids on the Aleutians in 1943, p. 89

Pearl Harbor, Hawaiian Islands
  Faulty handling of 5-inch shells causes loss of amphibious landing craft and almost postpones Marianas campaign, p. 128;

cruiser Northampton (CA-26) among first overhauled at the navy yard in the late 1930s, p. 49; Libby speculates on roles and culpability of key U.S. figures involved in December 1941 attack, pp. 229-233, 236

Pelelieu
Description of terrain, pp. 132, 134, 140; Guadalcanal used by Americans to practice for amphibious landing, p. 133

Pennsylvania, USS (BB-38)
Difficulty refueling the Pennsylvania using a towline brings about refinement in the process in 1943, pp. 93-94

Permanent Joint Board of Defense, U.S.-Canada
Origin and function, pp. 169-176

Phelps, USS (DD-360)
Flagship of Destroyer Squadron One was the only ship with radar in 1943, p. 83; Japanese torpedo plane mistakes the Phelps for a cruiser and sets the torpedoes too low to do any damage, in action off the Aleutians, pp. 90-91; movies shown aboard, pp. 91-92; patrolling in the Bering Sea, pp. 92-94; see also Destroyer Squadron One

Polaris Program
Development in the mid-1950s under Rear Admiral Raborn, pp. 215-216

Pound, Sir Dudley
Dissatisfaction with the lack of fleetness of the British Army, p. 67

Prisoners of War
Discussed during Korean War truce talks, pp. 183, 185, 188-191; U.S. Army general in charge of captured Communists in Korean War is taken by his prisoners and when released, demoted, p. 205; see also Repatriation

Raborn, Rear Admiral William F., Jr., USN (USNA, 1928)
Instrumental in development of Polaris program, pp. 215-216

Radar
Elementary nature of radar on Destroyer Squadron One flagship, USS Phelps, pp. 83-85; see also "Battle of the Pips"

Redstone Missiles
Army protects program against Air Force usurpment in the late 1940s, p. 163; Navy felt these missiles were undesirable for new subs that eventually were armed with Polaris missiles, p. 215

Refueling
   Mishap on New Mexico while attempting to refuel Concord in the mid-1930s, pp. 43-44; techniques refined during Aleutians campaign, pp. 93-94; sluggishness of Navy-chartered civilian tanker crew during refueling in the Aleutians, pp. 99-100

Repatriation
   Issue of voluntary repatriation of Communist prisoners of war complicated Korean War truce talks, pp. 189-194

Richardson, Admiral James O., USN (USNA, 1902)
   Relieved in 1941 for refusing to go along with basing of fleet at Pearl Harbor, p. 232

Rickover, Lieutenant Hyman C., USN (USNA, 1922)
   As assistant engineering officer on the New Mexico in the late 1930s, fiercely competitive desire to win engineering E evidenced during refueling, pp. 43-45; Libby debunks myth of Rickover's singlehanded development of nuclear power over great objections, pp. 233-236

Ridgway, General Matthew B., USA (USMA, 1917)
   As Commander in Chief, U.N. Command during the Korean War, relationship with U.S. negotiators, p. 192

Rigel, USS (AD-13)
   As station ship at San Diego in the early 1930s, commanding officer Nimitz and his family lived aboard, p. 4

Rock, Captain George H., USN (USNA, 1889)
   Senior naval construction officer enters letter on Libby's military record critical of his departure from that field in the early 1920s, pp. 30-31

Roosevelt, Franklin D.
   Relations with Churchill, pp. 68, 75-76; assessed by Libby, pp. 68-69; Libby speculates on prior knowledge of Pearl Harbor attack, pp. 230, 232-233, 236

Russell, Commander George L., USN (USNA, 1921B)
   As Admiral Ernest King's flag secretary during World War II, usually accompanied him on trips to the West Coast, p. 239

Saipan
   1944 invasion characterized as laborious, pp. 118-122; 8-inch Japanese gun destroyed by USS Tennessee (BB-43), pp. 127-128

Savo (August 1942)
   Unfamiliarity with area contributed to our defeat, p. 138

Seasickness
   Libby suffers aboard the Macdonough due to rolling tendency of ship, p. 39

Shells, Phosphorus
   Used by Newcomb at Pelelieu landing in 1944, p. 134

Signalling--Visual
   Difficulty seeing flags against setting sun during escort duty to Wake Island in 1943, pp. 102-103

Smoot, Commodore Roland N., USN (USNA, 1923)
   Relieves Libby as Commander Destroyer Squadron 56 and immediately leads squadron in Surigao Strait action, p. 141; as chief of officer detailing at the Bureau of Naval Personnel, called by Libby after his cruiser division was dissolved in 1946, p. 152

Sonar
   Use in the Aleutians operating area in 1943, pp. 96-97

Soviet Union
   Discussed at Casablanca Conference in 1942, p. 73; Murmansk convoys ceased, p. 73; Joint Strategic Survey Committee predicted need for strong hand with Soviet Union prior to end of World War II, p. 144; influence on Korean War, pp. 188-189

Stalin, Josef
   Uncooperative in discussions with Allies, p. 73

Stark, Admiral Harold R., USN (USNA, 1903)
   Mrs. Libby gets a call from Chief of Naval Operations Stark's secretary saying that Libby is safe in England, without saying what had happened, p. 52; loyalty of CNO King manifests itself in the Distinguished Service Medal Stark received at the end of the war, pp. 228-229; assessed as CNO in the early 1940s, p. 229; culpability for Pearl Harbor attack, pp. 229, 231-233, 236

Stoddert, USS (DD-302)
   Used for target practice in the early 1930s, p. 37

Strategy
   Libby assesses Pacific war strategy used during World War II, pp. 137-140; see Orange War Plan

Struble, Vice Admiral Arthur D., USN (USNA, 1915)
   As Chief of Naval Operations Denfeld's operational deputy, dealt with the Joint Chiefs of Staff in the late 1940s, pp. 168-169

Sullivan, John L.
  Resigns as Navy Secretary in 1949 when Defense Secretary Johnson cancels the building of the carrier United States, p. 167

Supply Corps -- U.S. Navy
  Renown for difficulty to deal with prior to World War II, p. 48

Talk Between Ships
  See TBS

Tarawa
  Difficult and unknown conditions prior to U.S. action in November 1943, pp. 107-108

Target Planning
  For close gunfire support during World War II, pp. 114-115

Target Practice
  Aviators use USS Boggs (AG-19) and Stoddert (DD-302) for practice in the early 1930s, pp. 35-37

Target Ships
  Libby's assessment of value of, pp. 37-38; see Boggs, USS (AG-19); Utah, USS (BB-31); Stoddert, USS (DD-302)

Task Force 14
  Participation in attack on Wake Island in 1943, pp. 100-103

Task Force 32
  Staff officers during Palau operation in late 1943, pp. 131-132

TBS (Talk Between Ships)
  Used to warn Phelps about Japanese torpedo planes in the Aleutians, p. 90; used to identify U.S. ships prior to Gilbert Islands action, p. 104; "iffy" nature of radio, p. 105

Tennessee, USS (BB-43)
  Scores perfect hit on 8-inch Japanese gun on Saipan in 1944, pp. 127-128

38th Parallel
  Chosen at random by Joint War Plans Committee as the dividing line between U.S. and Russian responsibility in Korea towards the end of the World War II, pp. 142-143, 145-146

Thomas, Charles S.
   As Navy Secretary in the mid-1950s, golf skill shown up by first-timer General Curtis Lemay, p. 208; sets out to reorganize Navy Department, pp. 212-214; involvement in Polaris program, p. 215; rapidly promotes Rear Admiral Felt, p. 216; has CNO Burke remove Vice Admiral "Wu" Duncan, p. 212

Tinian
   Ease of 1944 invasion and occupation after the fall of Saipan, pp. 118, 125; Japanese chose to die rather than surrender to the Americans, pp. 122-124; Japanese attack on Norman Scott (DD-690) and Colorado, USS (BB-45), pp. 124-125; U.S. builds airfield, p. 125; young marine captures 18 Japanese in cave, pp. 129-130

Truman, Harry S.
   Efforts to reduce the armed forces in the late 1940s, p. 163

Turkey
   Libby makes official calls at Istanbul during rare snowstorm in the mid-1950s, p. 210

Turner, Major General Howard McM., USAF (USMA, 1924)
   As U.S. negotiator at Korean War truce talks, expert at horseshoes, pp. 195-196

Turner, Rear Admiral Richmond K., USN (USNA, 1908)
   As Commander, Task Force 52 prior to Gilberts action, trained transports in formation en route from Pearl Harbor, pp. 103-104; sends Libby to torpedo unidentified ships that turn out to be ours, p. 104; assessed by Libby as decisive, pp. 107, 129; advises Libby of destroyer missing from screen, which ends up being in the correct slot in another formation, p. 119; brilliant use of amphibious forces during Marianas campaign, p. 128; praised for role in Guadalcanal campaign, pp. 318-319

UDT
   See Underwater Demolition Team

Underwater Demolition Team
   Communicated with destroyers offering gunfire support while laying charges off beach at Palau in 1943, pp. 117-118

United Nations Command
   Discussion of U.S. participation, under U.N. Command, in Korean War truce talks, pp. 182-210

United States, USS (CVA-58)
   See Sullivan, John L.

Utah, USS (BB-31)
  Used as a radio-controlled target in the 1930s, p. 37

Vandenberg, General Hoyt S., USAF (USMA, 1923)
  Assessed as first Chief of Staff of the Air Force in the mid-1940s, pp. 161-162

Visual Signalling
  Difficulty seeing flags against setting sun during escort duty to Wake Island in 1943, pp. 102-103

Wake Island
  Destroyer Squadron One escorts carrier task force to attack in 1943, p. 100

Wallace, Henry A.
  Libby's opinion of Wallace as War Production Board representative from his viewpoint as Admiral King's aide, p. 59

Wasp, USS (DV-18)
  Escorted by Destroyer Squadron 56 to Trinidad for shakedown in 1944, almost goes into mine field because navigator was using wrong information, pp. 109-110

Weapons -- Naval
  Mechanics of aiming shells, p. 135; see also Flame throwers; Redstone Missile; Shells, Phosphorus

Weather
  See: Foul Weather

Wedemeyer, Lieutenant General Albert C., USA (USMA, 1919)
  Strong backer of France defends deGaulle's position vis a vis Churchill and Roosevelt, pp. 63-64

Williwaw
  Unusual wind conditions around Aleutians causes problems during fleet exercise in late 1930s, p. 42

Willson, Rear Admiral Russell, USN (USNA, 1906)
  As member of the Joint Strategic Survey Committee at the end of World War II, p. 144

Wilson, Charles E.
  Defense Secretary in the mid-1950s initiates seminars at Quantico to get top Washington officials and military together, pp. 207-208

Wilson, Rear Admiral Henry B., USN (USNA, 1881)
   Naval Academy superintendent supports Libby in his switch from
   naval construction to line duty in the early 1920s, p. 29

Yeomans, Rear Admiral Elmer E., USN (USNA, 1924)
   As Commandant, Twelfth Naval District in 1963, invites the
   Nimitzes to move into quarters at Yerba Buena, pp. 12-13

www.ingramcontent.com/pod-product-compliance
Lightning Source LLC
Chambersburg PA
CBHW080615170426
43209CB00007B/1441